...er than Medical Degrees on such conditions as the said Chancellor Vice Chancellor a...

...and restrictions herein contained

...improvement of Medical education in all its branches as well in Medicine as in Surge...

...llor and Fellows shall from time to time report to one of our principal Secretaries of State coll...

...Medical Institutions and Schools in this Country or in Foreign parts as may be fit and expedient as...

...such report to be approved by our said Secretary And that no person shall be admitted as candidate...

...university unless they shall satisfy the said Chancellor Vice Chancellor and Fellows that such persons...

...said Chancellor Vice Chancellor and Fellows by regulation in that behalf shall determine and it...

...one of our principal Secretaries of State to vary alter and amend any such reports by striking out...

...ve power after examination to confer the several degrees of Bachelor Master and Doctor in Arts Laws Sciences...

...ice Chancellor and Fellows by regulations in that behalf shall from time to time determine And...

...and Fellows with the approbation of the Commissioners of our Treasury shall from time to time direct...

...the Examiners shall declare the name of every Candidate whom they shall have deemed to be entitled to any of...

...ime to time determine and he shall receive from the said Chancellor a Certificate under the Seal of the said...

...with the Degree taken by him shall be stated together with such other particulars if any as the said Chancellor...

...shall also have power to confer any of the said Degrees as Ad Eundem Degrees but no Degree so conferred...

...t of Incorporation

...ave power after examination to grant Certificates of Proficiency in such branches of Knowledge as the said...

...that in addition to the examination of Candidates for Degrees in this our Charter mentioned and ordained the...

...ll have prosecuted the study of such branches of Knowledge and who shall be candidates for such Certificates...

...shall from time to time be made in that behalf And on every such examination the Candidates shall be...

...ion of every examination of the Candidates the Examiner shall declare the name of every Candidate...

...id Chancellor Vice Chancellor and Fellows shall from time to time determine and he shall receive from...

...or in his absence or incapacity by the Vice Chancellor in which the branch or branches of Knowledge...

...as the said Chancellor Vice Chancellor and Fellows shall deem fitting to be stated therein and such reasonable...

...the approbation of the Commissioners of our Treasury shall from time to time direct...

...the payment of the expenses of the said University under the directions and regulations of the Commissioners of our...

...accounts shall be subject to such examination and audit as the said Commissioners may direct...

...reinbefore mentioned shall be submitted to one of our principal Secretaries of State and approved of...

...ese Our Letters patent or the enrolment or exemplification thereof shall be and by all things valid...

...and adjudged in the most favorable and beneficial sense for the University as well in our Courts as...

...tent In witness whereof we have caused these Our Letters to be made patent _ xa

...twenty first year of Our reign _

Command

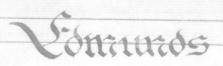

Edmunds

SENATE HOUSE LIBRARY
UNIVERSITY OF LONDON

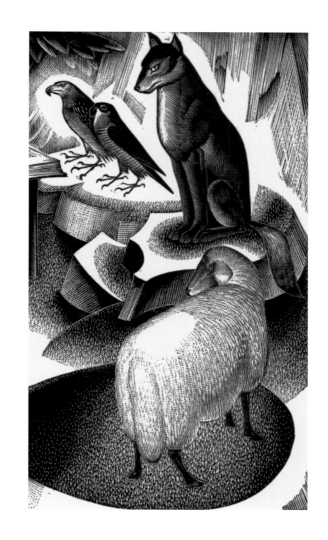

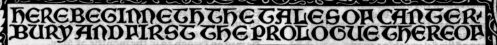

HERE BEGINNETH THE TALES OF CANTERBURY AND FIRST THE PROLOGUE THEREOF

The tendre croppes, and the yonge sonne
Hath in the Ram his halfe cours yronne,
And smale foweles maken melodye,
That slepen al the nyght with open eye,
So priketh hem nature in hir corages;
Thanne longen folk to goon on pilgrimages,
And palmeres for to seken straunge strondes,
To ferne halwes, kowthe in sondry londes;
And specially, from every shires ende
Of Engelond, to Caunterbury they wende,
The hooly blisful martir for to seke,
That hem hath holpen whan that they were
seeke.

Bifil that in that seson on a day,
In Southwerk at the Tabard as
I lay,
Redy to wenden on my pilgrym-
age
To Caunterbury with ful devout
corage,
At nyght were come into that hostelrye
Wel nyne and twenty in a compaignye,
Of sondry folk, by aventure yfalle
In felaweshipe, and pilgrimes were they alle,
That toward Caunterbury wolden ryde.

THAT Aprille with his shoures soote
The droghte of March hath perced to the roote,
And bathed every veyne in swich licour,
Of which vertu engendred is the flour;
Whan Zephirus eek with his swete breeth
Inspired hath in every holt and heeth

SENATE HOUSE LIBRARY
UNIVERSITY OF LONDON

Edited by Christopher Pressler and Karen Attar

SCALA

Contents

Introduction: We Are All Shakespeare

Senate House Library was designed to stand at the centre of the third great English university. It was to be a university rooted in the contemporary world, and at home only in the world's capital.

The nature of humanities research still requires engagement with, and the development of, large physical collections. Research libraries in the broader humanities, though, are not merely stores. A research project is a partnership between the researcher and the library from the earliest survey of current materials, through the interpretation of materials or digital environments, finally to the placement of that research in the setting of the library. Research is concerned with discovery. Libraries are the essential mode of travel.

At Senate House Library these journeys are made in central London, as part of the greatest concentration of libraries anywhere in the world. In 1936 the architect of Senate House, Charles Holden, began building this Art Deco masterpiece. The library is designed to be a building that would stand naturally only in London. There are echoes of the lives of other great universities, such as in the inclusion of cloisters, but Holden did not design *faux*-medieval or classical copies. The cloisters at Senate House are new ideas.

Perhaps the most striking infrastructural feature of the building is its least known. Senate House can only ever be a library. From Floor 7 to Floor 19 the supporting mechanism for this, London's first skyscraper, is bookshelves. They are welded into the skeleton girders and rise in perfect symmetry for about 200 feet over the city.

For a research library of the intellectual depth of Senate House, no detail should be considered too small. That the collections are held in a building formed from design principles of modernist simplicity affords an important opportunity. Senate House confirms its function and usability by adhering to those principles. Integrity is derived through clearly stating purpose. The purpose of Senate House was made physical by Holden and will be secured for the future by allowing the objects and designs of the contemporary world to integrate with their Art Deco surroundings. Every technology, every sight-line, every website, every product and every service in such an important building needs to be considered in terms of design, as something people interact with.

*

One of the finest characteristics of humans is our ability to share. In the academic library context this has meant, and is still defined by, libraries' contributions to the archiving and rediscovery of human action.

At the heart of all universities, the library in its many facets continues to balance tensions between print and digital collections, between the demands of teaching and research, between the arts and sciences, and, perhaps most importantly, between the commercial supply of research information and support for its creation in academic practice.

Libraries are present at the generation of ideas, in delivering content to the desktop and the desk top. They deliver in perpetuity for results and theories. Libraries bring people into contact with innovation, with innovators and with each other. They draw an inconceivably long line of thought in every discipline to the minds of current thinkers. Libraries are critical in our need to share and to discover. They are vital in allowing access to our recorded thoughts by those who follow us.

The ancient ideal of a library was handed down from ruler to ruler, from society to society, across cultures until it arrived in Alexandria – the great iconic library of the past. The Alexandrian library was also 'global', containing manuscripts from throughout the known world. Smaller, certainly, than our own world collection, but then the world too was smaller and less known then.

I believe we share with ancient culture an understanding of the role of the library as knowledge passed from generation to generation. It may happen faster and in more ways now, but information was a shared, precious and powerful commodity in antiquity as it is for us. Texts were carried from past to present, and it is this narrative, unbroken and incorruptible, that gives the library its power and validity. In antiquity the very act of collecting, of bringing together many texts, injected into each book an added command over the population. The early library was the material meaning of the phrase 'safety in numbers'.

*

Jorge Luis Borges, in his miniature story about Shakespeare called *Everything and Nothing*, describes how, when Shakespeare meets God, the poet says, 'I who have been so many men in vain want to be one and myself.' The voice of the Lord answers from a whirlwind: 'Neither am I anyone; I have dreamt the world as you dreamt your work, my Shakespeare, and among the forms in my dream are you, who like myself are many and no one.' In Borges's last story,

Shakespeare's Memory, a man is given the entire mind of the poet. As it gradually overwhelms him, he passes it on. Borges believed that the words of one man are the words of all men, and that the construct of the library is where they are to be found. In the library we are all Shakespeare.

Borges believed art to be an essential force and the library to be a labyrinth. To Borges, libraries remain linked to dreams, to memory, to political freedom, to educational opportunity and to truth.

Those of us presently caring for the collections at Senate House Library are pleased to present a selection of rare materials in this, a book of books. I would like to thank my colleagues at the library, in particular Dr Karen Attar, and also all of our distinguished contributors for their role in producing this path through one of the world's most significant collections.

Christopher Pressler FRSA
Director of Senate House Libraries,
University of London

Above: UoL/SV/V/36, Senate House and Library from the south-west

Left: UoL/SV/V/36, the Goldsmiths' Library

Opposite: UoL/SV/V/36, the south window in the Goldsmiths' Library

Senate House Library: The First Hundred Years

The beginnings

The University of London was founded by Royal Charter in 1836 (see no. 34). It was established purely as an examining body, not for teaching purposes. Thus, unlike its precursors, University College (founded 1826) and King's College (founded 1831), it did not begin life with a library. Nonetheless, book provision began with over 200 books on diverse subjects given to the University in 1838. From then on, a steady trickle of books came in, on subjects ranging from medicine to Old Norse romance, largely donations by authors or learned societies of their own works. The first record of a purchase occurs in Senate Minutes from 1839; the second in December 1846. The latter includes the first known reference to the University Library: 'That the Treasurer be authorized to purchase for the University Library, Rutherford's "Institutes" and Dumont's "Traités du Code Civil, et du Code Pénal", in which works Candidates for the Degree of B.L. are examined.'

The impetus for a library proper was the University's move from a house in Savile Row to its first purpose-built accommodation in Burlington Gardens, Piccadilly, in 1870. On 15 March 1871 the Liberal politician Julian Goldsmid, later to become Vice-Chancellor of the University, wrote to current Vice-Chancellor George Grote:

You know that I have taken great interest in two things which I, in common with many others, thought of vital importance to the University of London, the one being the acquiring a University Building, *and the other* obtaining Representation in Parliament. *Both these questions being settled, it appears to me that there is one other object we should now have in view, and that is the establishment of a first-class University Library, which I think will not only improve the position of the University, but also be of great service to its Students and Graduates.*

Goldsmid accordingly gave the University £1,000 (equivalent to at least £45,700 at a twenty-first-century reckoning), at the rate of £100 a year over ten years, to purchase Classical books. His generosity inspired more. A mere fortnight after the death of mathematician and mathematical historian Augustus De Morgan on 18 March 1871, a paragraph appeared in *The Spectator* wondering about the fate of De Morgan's library and suggesting that it would be a worthy addition to the University of London. Samuel Loyd, Baron Overstone, a member of the University Senate,

accordingly purchased the books and presented them to the University, writing to the Senate in June 1871:

It is a source of satisfaction to me to have been the means of preventing the disperssion [sic] *of this remarkable collection of mathematical Works; and I gladly present it to the London University, as a testimony of my appreciation of the service which that Body has rendered to the extension and improvement of Education in all its branches throughout the United Kingdom, and in the hope that it may prove the first fruits of a Library which shall ere long become such in all respects as the London University ought to possess.*

De Morgan had bought as extensively as he could with limited means. The gift of his collection gave the University Library an estimated 3,000 titles, some apparently unique, concerning the various branches of mathematics, its history and astronomy (see nos. 5, 33, 40). Obvious treasures included the first five printed editions of Euclid, first editions of Newton's *Principia* and *Opticks*, and Copernicus's *De Revolutionibus*, this last individualised by De Morgan's annotations;[1] also noteworthy were runs of popular textbooks, such as *Cocker's Arithmetic* and Francis Walkingame's *The Tutor's Assistant*. De Morgan's notes, often humorous and sometimes shedding light on the history of mathematics, enhanced a significant minority of the books. His collection gave the Library its first 'special collection' (not that it was so designated at the time) and a noteworthy injection of antiquarian books: approximately 1,380 printed between the fifteenth and eighteenth centuries.

On 18 June 1871, just four months after De Morgan, the London Vice-Chancellor and Classical historian George Grote died, bequeathing his books to the University (see nos. 8, 44). Unlike De Morgan, Grote had not been a conscious collector. But he had been a voracious reader, with money from 1830 onwards to satisfy his wide-ranging literary interests. His library contained about 5,000 titles, beginning with the Heber copy of an Aldine publication, Ammonius Hermiae's *Hypomnēma eis to peri ermēnias Aristotelous* (1503) and a 1504 edition of Gregor Reisch's *Margarita Philosophica* (see no. 8) and ranging from works on economics, mathematics and English history from the seventeenth century to nineteenth-century German philosophy and literature.

The De Morgan and Grote Libraries constituted the University Library's founding collections. Their receipt

Practise, named PANTOMETRIA,
diuided into three Bookes, *Longimetra,*
Planimetra and *Stereometria*, containing Rules manifolde
for menſuration of all lines, Superficies and Solides: with
ſundꝛy ſtraunge concluſions both by inſtrument
and without, and alſo by Perſpectiue glaſſes, to
ſet foꝛth the true deſcription oꝛ exact plat of
an whole Region : framed by *Leonard*
Digges Gentleman, lately finiſhed
by Thomas Digges his
ſonne.

Who hathe alſo thereunto adioyned a *Mathematicall* treatiſe of
the ſiue regulare *Platonicall* bodies, and their *Metamorphoſis*
oꝛ tranſfoꝛmation into ſiue other equilater vnifoꝛme
ſolides *Geometricall*, of his owne inuention, hitherto not mentioned of by any *Geometricians.*

2000 paſe

1500 paſe

Imprinted at London by Henrie Bynneman.
ANNO. 1571.

attracted more gifts, both of books and of money. Whereas previous donations had been primarily of single titles, in 1871 the Master of Rolls wrote to offer the University over 270 volumes, with a complete set of the Royal Society's *Philosophical Transactions* deposited by the Society in 1876. In 1871 the Chancellor empowered the Registrar to provide £25 annually for ten years for Library books, and the Member of Parliament authorised him to give £50 to buy scientific books. From 1873, as noted in the Library's first catalogue, the Library received an annual Treasury grant of £100, which met current expenditure and left a slender balance to purchase new works. Moreover, in 1871 a committee was appointed from among the members of the Senate, including such distinguished figures as the historian Lord Acton and the politician Sir William Stirling Maxwell, to purchase Library books and prepare Library regulations. Purchases were made in most subsequent years, with varying levels of funds, and an emphasis on

books taken from the lists now submitted to, or from lists previously approved by, the Committee, with such additions thereto as may seem advisable in order to obtain the latest and best editions of Classical authors and to improve the collection of Dictionaries and other standard works of reference now in the Library, preference being given to such works as from cost, rarity, or otherwise, may not be generally accessible to students. (Senate Minute 76, 30 March 1881)

Graduates of the University were the main constituency. A Senate resolution of April 1874 refers to the Library as a physical space: 'That the Library be not used, except under special circumstances, for other Examinations than those held by the University'.

In 1872 it was decided that the Assistant Registrar should undertake the duties of Librarian, with a messenger to act as his assistant. Also in 1872, Thomas Nichols, an employee of the British Museum, was appointed to create a Library catalogue. The resulting short-title catalogue, 795 pages long, appeared in 1876. It contained books in the Library by the end of 1875, and indicated the source of books when this was Augustus De Morgan, George Grote, the East India Office (147 volumes) or the Public Record Office. Locations were not supplied. A supplementary catalogue, prepared by R. W. Chambers (subsequently Librarian of University College London, and an impressive literary scholar), was published in 1900, summarising the content of the earlier catalogue and extending it to the end of 1897.

The Library opened in 1877. Library regulations allowed for Members of the Senate, Members of Convocation and other persons duly recommended by them to borrow six volumes for a loan period of three months; not until 1907 could teachers of the University borrow books.

UoL/UL/12/22, Herbert Somerton Foxwell, founder of the Goldsmiths' Library of Economic Literature

The Imperial Institute

In 1900 the University Library moved with the rest of the administrative portion of the University of London to the Imperial Institute in South Kensington. Here, three years later, it received the collection that would have most impact on its future development. Herbert Somerton Foxwell (1849–1936) had laid the foundations for an academic library with the purchase of Dionysus Lardner's *Railway Economy* in about 1875 (see no. 38) and had begun collecting seriously in the 1880s, initially with the aim of providing material for a historical edition, never completed, of *The Wealth of Nations*, and expanding to cover works on the

Note by Foxwell on Lardner, *Railway Economy* (1850), the founding item of the Goldsmiths' Library of Economic Literature

I bought this volume from a bookstall in Great Portland Street at Jevons' suggestion, one afternoon as I was going to Hampstead with him, for 6d.!

He urged me to buy it, partly on account of the low price, partly because it was a book of great intrinsic value, & one which had suggested to him the mathematical treatment of economic theory. [cf. ch. xiii.]

This purchase was the first step in the formation of my economic collection. circ. 1875.   H.S.F.

Industrial Revolution, 1760–1860, currency and banking history, and ultimately economics generally, with a particular effort for completeness as far as English economic history was concerned. Like De Morgan, Foxwell was an academic with modest means. Upon his marriage in 1898, he resolved to sell his collection of some 30,000 items, on the basis that he could not afford to maintain both a book collection and a wife. The John Crerar Library in Chicago expressed interest in buying it. On 25 June 1901 *The Times* appealed: 'Is it right that PROFESSOR FOXWELL's unequalled collection of economic literature should be carried away from the country of ADAM SMITH, ARTHUR YOUNG, and RICARDO by some foreigner who is able to draw a big cheque?', and suggested that the collection 'might, perhaps, find a fitting home in the new London University'. Just two days later the Worshipful Company of Goldsmiths paid the requisite £10,000, and in 1903 the books, broadsides (see no. 23), pamphlets and manuscripts entered the University Library, instantly doubling its holdings. Until 1913 Foxwell continued to select material to be added to the collection (see no. 3), with funds provided by the Goldsmiths' Company.

When the Goldsmiths' Library arrived, the University Library was in a state of chaos. Funds remained meagre. Books were arranged haphazardly and scattered; the Principal and the Secretary to the Finance Committee occupied rooms intended for the Library; and, as a deputation from Convocation complained: 'There is no Librarian, and it is purely a matter of chance whether any book asked for can be unearthed.' Consequently, in 1904 the University of London appointed its first Librarian, initially intended to be a temporary employee for a year, at a salary of £150, to catalogue the University Library and the Goldsmiths' Library (seen as distinct entities for decades to come) and to take charge of both, 'with the object of bringing both into working order as soon as possible'. Sidney Webb, founder of the London School of Economics and a member of the Library Committee, hoped thereby 'to have a really efficient organisation of a University Library worthy of London & covering the whole field & work of the University as a whole with an adequate salary for a Chief Librarian of organising capacity & high standing'. He recommended appointing a woman:

You will get a far better woman for £150 than a man. For this sum you could get a good University-educated, practically competent woman, who would regard the job as a valuable prize [...] A man at that price would be either a callow youth, who would leave us at the first chance; or a half-educated clerk; or a 'failure' without energy or grit.

One woman, from the London School of Economics, and one man were interviewed. The man, Lawrence Warrington Haward, B.A., was chosen. The Library was closed for cataloguing and organisation to take place.

The year's contract was extended, and in 1905 Haward was joined by Reginald Arthur Rye, in the new role of Assistant Librarian. The next year Haward resigned, and Rye replaced him.

The Library was opened formally in its new quarters by the Chancellor of the University, Archibald Primrose, fifth Earl of Rosebery, on 26 October 1906. In many ways its time in the Imperial Institute was marked by tribulation. It included a constant fight for recognition: 'The Library is at present very little known even to Members of the University', wrote Rye in a memorandum of 1908, and again in 1910: 'It is thought that many students at the Colleges and Schools of the University are unaware of the facilities which are provided for them at the University Library.' Insufficient space, a complaint from early days in the Institute, intensified with time. Books spread everywhere, even to the kitchens, with some books tellingly shelf-marked 'canteen cupboards'. The Library Committee report for 1924 ended: 'In every branch of the Library's work waste of labour and serious obstacles to further development are caused by lack of sufficient room both for the books and the Library Staff.' Moreover, the very existence of the Library was threatened when, in 1913, a Royal Commission report recommended moving the Goldsmiths' Library to the London School of Economics, and, should the University remain at South Kensington, dispersing and distributing among the Colleges of the University of London the general holdings of the University Library. The University countered that transplanting the Goldsmiths' Library would involve a breach of trust, and that dispersal among the Colleges would be prejudicial to general access.

Yet the period in the Imperial Institute was marked by remarkable growth, celebrated to an extent by published catalogues of works of palaeography, proclamations, broadsides and of manuscripts and autograph letters.[2] In 1908 the University, using Goldsmiths' Company funding, purchased the collection of the railway engineer John Urpeth Rastrick (see no. 37), comprising his early notebooks, plans and estimates, as well as a large number of early pamphlets on English, American and Italian railways. Other important accessions included 4,000 items for the Goldsmiths' Library, described as comprising some of the most valuable books in the Library, sent by Foxwell in 1912; approximately 2,500 volumes of Parliamentary Papers 1816–78 given by the Reform Club in 1923; and the gift in 1913 of the Lady Welby Library, about 2,000 nineteenth- and early twentieth-century books and pamphlets on philosophy, philology, economics and education, remarkable for Lady Welby's extensive notes and annotations. The year 1921 saw the Library's most important single acquisition, a fourteenth-

century manuscript recounting the life of the Black Prince (see no. 1), presented by the University to Edward, Prince of Wales, when conferring upon him the honorary degrees of Master of Commerce and Doctor of Science, and placed on permanent loan by him in the University Library.

The year 1929 was significant as the only one in the Library's history to see the acquisition of two significant named special collections. The Quick Memorial Library, given by the Education Guild, was based on the library formed by the educationalist Robert Hebert Quick (1831–1891), and was devoted largely to the history of education (see nos. 14, 24, 35). Its thousand or so books, including ninety volumes of bound pamphlets, embraced the theory and practice of education, textbooks from the sixteenth century onwards, and children's books. It contributed numerous rare items. Valuable as it was, it was dwarfed by the larger Durning-Lawrence Library (see nos. 15,

16, 19, 20, 28 and 29), which contained more obviously stellar items, such as the first four Shakespeare folios and the Coverdale Bible, and enjoyed a much more visible presence from 1938 onwards through having its own dedicated room, built to incorporate the furnishings from its previous home in Carlton House Terrace. The Durning-Lawrence Library was the collection of Sir Edwin Durning-Lawrence (1837–1929), a wealthy one-time Member of Parliament best known for his prolific and vehement support of the Baconian theory of Shakespearean authorship. According to Sir Edwin's widow, Edith (the donor), every one of its estimated 5,700 items 'was purchased with one aim, and that aim was to prove that Francis Bacon was at the head of a great literary and scientific society, from whence emanated all the Elizabethan and Jacobean literature'. The library was rich not only in early editions of the works of Sir Francis Bacon but in all areas with which, according to the most catholic

DLL/4/15, the interior of the library formed by Sir Edwin Durning-Lawrence at Carlton House Terrace, London

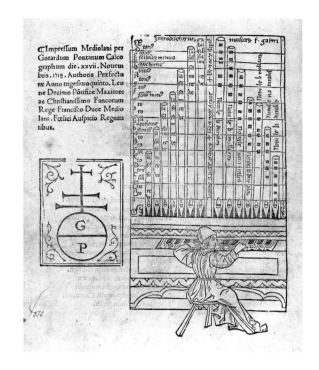

views of Baconian authorship, Bacon could be connected: literary works, emblem books, rare Rosicrucian texts, and Bibles. It gave the University of London Library its first great literary collection and sowed the seed for strong Shakespearean holdings.

Larger again was the intake from the London Institution (founded in 1805 with the primary object of developing a library), most of whose 150,000 books passed into the possession of the University of London when it closed its doors in Finsbury Circus in 1910. The oriental books formed the nucleus of the School of Oriental and African Studies library, and over several years the University of London Library, University College London and King's College London divided up the rest. The University Library was the recipient of particularly sumptuous books (see nos. 9, 18, 26 and 36) and also of the rump, taken because Rye, fully intending to discard the books, wanted to use the number of linear feet they occupied to negotiate for additional Library space. Their intake was responsible for much of the overcrowding in the Imperial Institute, but also for an influx of antiquarian holdings across all subject areas which considerably enriched the Library.

In 1924 the Senate of the University of London charged a special Music Committee to make recommendations about the place of music in the University's curriculum and social life. The result was the establishment of a music library, which opened in December 1926 in a room in the roof of the London Institution, complete with pianola and gramophone. Founding items included 470 titles comprising the music collection of the organist and composer Sir George Job Elvey

(1816–1893), placed in the Library on permanent loan by Elvey's son. Two notable consequent gifts followed in 1932 from the Carnegie United Kingdom Trust: approximately 20,000 sheets of photostatic reproductions of printed and manuscript Tudor and Jacobean music, and the much smaller Littleton Collection (see no. 11), comprising twenty-seven titles from the fifteenth to the seventeenth centuries purchased at the auction in 1918 of the library of Alfred Henry Littleton (1845–1914), Chairman of the music publishing house Novello. Despite its numerical smallness, the gift was significant in that every item in it was rare and was a landmark in music printing. Significant, too, was the consciousness of the University Library which prompted the donation, offered on the suggestion of Sir Percy Buck, King Edward Professor of Music at the University of London and himself a donor to the music library, as: 'It is probable that there is no place quite so suitable for them as your Department', an institution with 'plenty of shelf room, ample space for study and expert custodianship'.

Senate House

The Library was not the only part of the University of London to find conditions at South Kensington trying. The building was cramped and uncomfortable generally, and the location was too remote for a University which required a high visible profile. Accordingly, in

1926, after lengthy dithering, it was decided to move the University administration and the Library to Bloomsbury. Senate House was constructed between 1932 and 1937 (see no. 59).

Most of the central University moved into the still unfinished Senate House in 1936. The University Library was transferred in 1937 and 1938, working at a split site over those years. The Library entrance was on the fourth floor of the new Senate House, and this floor gave access to readers and contained the reading rooms. These included a room for maps and palaeography, areas which it had been decided to promote in the new Library. The fifth, sixth and seventh floors were book stacks. The music library was on the fifth floor; the theses room and the Harry Price Room, to house a collection in the process of being deposited, were on the seventh. From within the library, a staircase connected with the Periodicals Room on the third floor and the travelling libraries department, which sent books out for extension and extra-mural courses, on the second. At the time, the University Library held about 337,300 volumes and pamphlets. Room was provided for about 600,000 volumes and 300 readers, with the possibility of extension. The Goldsmiths' Company financed a reading room for its library, the County of Middlesex two others.

Conditions in Senate House were not, in fact, ideal. One employee recorded that the lift for fetching books from the tower was 'absurdly small and very slow moving', and that poor lighting in the galleries of two reading rooms after dark 'made it extremely difficult to locate books on the lower two shelves', while 'the artificial lighting in the Goldsmiths' Library was so unsatisfactory that it was seriously suggested that electric torches should be used to help find books situated in the many dark corners'; his summary was that Senate House would 'always suffer to a certain extent from being monumental rather than functional'. However, the readers' guide of 1939 noted proudly the steel frame of the tower, the steel shelving of the stacks, the English walnut furniture of the reading rooms and the decorative ceiling, panelled in South American cypress wood, of the Goldsmiths' Library. Above all, the added space was beneficial.

The pristine new building did not remain pristine for long. When war broke out, College teaching was scattered across Great Britain, while the University of London's central administration moved first to Royal Holloway College in Surrey and then, in 1941, to Richmond. The Library continued to function, although it was closed from May 1940 onwards to most personal visitors except staff from the wartime Ministry of Information, which occupied Senate House. It provided a reference library service to the Ministry of Information and similar institutions, and equipment from the music library assisted the BBC in raising morale. The Library was hit in five air raids,

Left: UoL/UL/12/28, unpacking stock at Senate House, 1937

most notably on 8 and 16 November 1940. Although few books were lost, windows, shelving and furnishings were smashed, walls crumbled, and roofs were no longer weatherproof. The most valuable material was stored in Senate House in metal boxes throughout the war. In 1941, 3,098 feet of books were evacuated to the Bodleian Library in Oxford, with another 400 boxes of books going to Cambridge. More positively, the war years saw a continued stream of donations, including Ministry publications and presents (see no. 58), and early printed books and others which became an encumbrance in private homes (see no. 25), besides which the Library took full advantage of low prices on the antiquarian book market (see no. 4).

After the war

In July 1944 (two years beyond retirement age, owing to the exigencies of war) Reginald Arthur Rye retired after thirty-eight years of service at the helm of the Library, during which holdings had expanded from about 35,000 to almost 377,000 items. John Henry Pyle Pafford, previously Sub-Librarian of the National Central Library and a lecturer at the School of Librarianship of University College London, succeeded him in October 1945 and remained for twenty-two years, until retirement in 1967.

According to Pafford's obituary in *The Independent*, 'he directed and promoted the growth of the university library into a notable centre of research and scholarship. On a budget that was never generous, he came near to doubling its holdings, and having accomplished its recovery from war damage, developed its premises to house great new collections which he helped to attract.' The first of the great new collections attracted in his time was offered in 1945 by the EMI magnate Sir Louis Sterling (1879–1958) (see nos. 2, 7,

Above: UoL/UL/12/3, University of London Library staff, 1949

Below: Original drawing by Thomas Rowlandson from the Sterling Library

"Walking fast and far: in a hot Sun: to overtake a woman: from whose shape and air as viewd en derriere you have decided that her Face is angelic. till on eagerly turning 'round as you pass her. you are petrified by a Gorgon.—

30, 32, 39, 43 and 46). This was a 'high spot' collection of 4,200 items of first and fine editions of English literature. Specific treasures included two Caxtons, the Doves Bible, Rowlandson drawings and a complete set of Kelmscott Press books, three Shakespeare quartos and all four folios, and Dickens parts among many others. In his introduction to the catalogue of the Library printed in 1954, Sterling explained:

On reaching the age of three score and ten I felt that I would like to make some useful disposition of my library and decided that in due course it should go as a gift to London University. I felt that the great city of London, to which I was inspired to emigrate from America a half-century before, had been good to me; and I hope that the gift of my library may be some acknowledgement of what London has given me.

The Sterling Library came to the University in 1956 and was opened ceremoniously by Queen Elizabeth, the Queen Mother, as Chancellor. Sterling hoped explicitly that his gift would inspire further generosity, and others indeed responded: Librarian J. H. P. Pafford, whose gifts to the Library over the years ranged from Pico della Mirandola's *Opera* (1496) to a group of eighty-one nineteenth-century prize books bought in charity shops (see no. 49), gave a collection of editions of the poetry of George Crabbe in 1982, while in 1965 Professor Sir David Hughes Parry (1893–1973), Vice-Chancellor of the University of London 1945–8 and Chairman of the University Court from 1962 to 1970, gave the Library a complete set of specially bound editions of books produced by the Gregynog Press (see no. 56), supplementing Sterling's collection of private press books.

Before the war, in 1936, the psychical researcher Harry Price had begun to deposit his collection of books, pamphlets and manuscripts on magical litera-ture – sleight of hand, psychic phenomena, witchcraft, demonology and other subjects – with the University, with accretions in subsequent years. When he died, in 1948, the deposit, numbering some 14,000 items from the fifteenth to the twentieth centuries, became a bequest (see nos. 6, 21, 41, 53 and 55). Price, who was not renowned for modesty, had described his collec-tion as 'the most complete library of magical literature in Great Britain, if not in Europe'. The more sober

Library Committee annual report for 1948 described the collection as 'one of the world's leading collections in its field'. It became one of the most distinctive and best used of the University Library.[3]

Meanwhile, the Library re-opened to users in August 1945, and it boomed. In contradistinction to earlier pessimistic views of the Library's prominence, the Library's 1947 annual report observed that the Library was becoming better known, a positive assessment repeated in 1956. It was certainly becoming well used. Hours of opening increased in the late 1940s and the 1950s to meet demand, and finding space for readers became a challenge; by 1965 it was estimated that space was required for 200 more readers. Post-war repairs to the building began in 1948 and continued into 1950. The palaeography room was separated from the map room in 1952. The newly re-shelved and refurbished palaeography room opened in 1956, and a periodicals room with nearby stack area, envisaged before the war, was completed in 1959.

Embroidered binding of a manuscript in the Harry Price Library: Joanna Southcott, 'The Christian's Robe of Faith', 1795

A particularly welcome development came in 1947, when the London County Council gave permission for the Senate House tower, hitherto an empty hulk, to be converted to book stacks, creating space for 300,000 more books. With the additional space came the capacity to take in additional donated and deposited collections. From the Guildhall came in 1956 the Elzevier Collection of 1,150 seventeenth-century Dutch imprints (gifted) and the Eliot-Phelips Collection of some 3,500 items of Hispanica formed by Edward Phelips (1882–1928) (deposited; see no. 17), described in *The Times* when it entered public ownership in 1928 as being unrivalled outside Spain. A special grant from the Senate enabled the purchase of some 7,000 volumes of Parliamentary Papers from the Reform Club in 1957. The Church of England deposited the library of the eighteenth-century Bishop of London Beilby Porteus (1731–1809), extending beyond theology to slavery and economics, among other subjects, in 1958; Jesus College, Cambridge, deposited the library of

Henry Trotter (d. 1766), the rector of Graveley parish, near Ely, in Cambridgeshire, in 1960. From 1957 onwards, the shorthand bibliographer William J. Carlton (1886–1973) began the gift of his collection of an estimated 18,000 books, periodicals, manuscripts, prints and pamphlets of or about shorthand, in nearly sixty languages and dialects dating from the sixteenth to the twentieth centuries (see no. 22) – one of the most comprehensive shorthand collections in the world. In 1964 came the gift of over 4,000 items pertaining to the history of London, ranging from the sixteenth to the twentieth centuries, collected by the co-founder of Gaumont Cinemas Lieutenant-Colonel Alfred Claude Bromhead (1876–1963) (see no. 13) – and these, albeit salient additions, were by no means the only ones. Gifts were especially welcome, as the prices of modern and especially antiquarian material were increasing sharply, such that year after year the Librarian bewailed the diminishing effect of book budgets. Storage space, however, again became

UoL/UL/12/41, the newly refurbished palaeography room, *c.* 1955 problematical. The University of London opened a co-operative depository store in Egham in 1961, and soon depended on sending quantities of lesser-used books to it annually in order to make way for new acquisitions.

Manuscripts and archives had continued to enter the Library steadily after the war. Acquisitions included the purchase, enabled by a special grant from the Senate and assistance from the Friends of the National Libraries, of the Ilchester Manuscript of *Piers Plowman* (the copy of the C-text transcribed and collated by Walter Skeat in 1873), in 1962; gifts of the literary remains of the writer Thomas Sturge Moore in 1964 (see no. 52); further Rastrick material in 1965; the personal correspondence of the Victorian social reformers Charles and Mary Booth in 1968; and donations across several years from the pianist Harriet Cohen, including letters from the actress Florence Farr and music manuscripts by Arnold Bax (see no. 57). An asset for research, if a logistical challenge in terms of space occupied, was the Library's assumption of responsibility in 1960 of a University Archive (see nos. 34, 45, 48, 54, 59 and 60). An influx of material soon followed, as University departments passed on what old documents had been retained.

Printed catalogues and descriptions of collections continued to be published over the years, most sumptuously *The Sterling Library: A Catalogue of the Printed Books and Literary Manuscripts Collected by Sir Louis Sterling and Presented by Him to the University of London* (privately printed, 1954). As the Library approached the hundredth anniversary of its opening, its most ambitious catalogue began to appear. Volume 1 of the *Catalogue of the Goldsmiths' Library of Economic Literature, Printed Books to 1800*, compiled by Margaret Canney and David Knott, appeared in 1970. Volume 2 (*Printed Books, 1801–1850*) followed in 1975, with a further three volumes covering additions to the printed books, periodicals and indices to come between 1982 and 1995. The catalogue turned the collection into a yardstick for economic literature, the phrase 'not in Goldsmiths' becoming a sign of rarity in booksellers' catalogues. A decision in 1972 to micro-film the material in the Goldsmiths' Library expanded a year later to become a collaborative project with the Kress Library at Harvard (Foxwell's second collection), one of the largest of its kind ever undertaken.[4]

When the Library attained its centenary in 1977, a major change lay in the immediate future. In the 1980s, under Douglas Foskett and V. T. H. Parry, it ceased by stages to collect in the natural sciences – always a small and perfunctory area of acquisition – in order to concentrate on the arts and social sciences, which had always been its strengths. Challenges would remain, but so would good will, growth and gifts (see nos. 12, 27, 51). The path was laid for it to enter its next century as a leading British humanities library.

Notes

1. Featured in David Pearson, *Books as History* (London: British Library, 2008), p. 131.

2. John Wilks and Arthur Douglas Lacey, *Catalogue of Works Dealing with the Study of Western Palæography in the Libraries of the University of London at its Central Buildings and at University College and at King's College* (London, 1921); [Arthur Douglas Lacey], *Catalogue of the Collection of English, Scottish and Irish Proclamations in the University Library (Goldsmiths' Library of Economic Literature) at the Central Building of the University of London* (London, 1928); [Arthur Douglas Lacey], *Catalogue of the Collection of Broadsides in the University Library (Goldsmiths' Library of Economic Literature) at the Central Building of the University of London* (London, 1930); Reginald Arthur Rye, *Catalogue of the Manuscripts and Autograph Letters in the University Library at the Central Building of the University of London* (London, 1921).

3. Between 2008 and 2010 much of its nineteenth-century content was digitised by Adam Matthew for the database *Victorian Popular Culture*.

4. In 2005 the microfilms became widely available when digitised by Gale Cengage as *The Making of the Modern Economy* (2005), soon renamed *The Making of the Modern World*.

Overleaf: UoL/SV/V/36, the Middlesex Library South

60
TREASURES

Chandos Herald, 'Edward, Prince of Wales, the Black Prince'

c. 1385

236 × 140 mm; MS1

This splendid monument to chivalry provides an eyewitness account in over 4,000 lines of French verse couplets of the exploits of Edward, the Black Prince (1330–1376), during the Hundred Years War. It was composed by the domestic herald of the soldier, administrator and follower of Edward, Sir John Chandos (d. 1370). The poem describes Edward III's French campaign of 1346, culminating in the Battle of Crécy (the first major engagement of the War), the capture of Calais in 1347 (with some details of the French plot to recover Calais in 1349) and the Battle of Poitiers (1356). It further provides an eyewitness account of the Spanish campaign of the Black Prince on behalf of Don Pedro of Castile, ending in the Battle of Nájera (1367). A summary follows of the end of the Black Prince's government in Gascony and the loss of possessions gained at Brétigny, then an account of the Prince's last years. After the poem comes a list of the Black Prince's chief officers in Aquitaine, and his epitaph in Canterbury Cathedral. The poem also occurs in a manuscript in Worcester College, Oxford.

To judge from the quality of the illumination, this may have been a presentation copy. It opens with a full-page miniature depicting the Holy Trinity. God the Father, enthroned, holds a crucifix, with the dove of the

1.1

1.1 detail of fol. 2r, with inscription of John Shirley

1.2 fol. 2v–3r, God the Father (above) and the Black Prince (below), and beginning of poem

1.3 detail of fol. 27v, with illuminated initial

1.2

Holy Spirit above. Below, the Black Prince kneels in prayer, his devotion to the Trinity indicated by a scroll issuing from his mouth bearing the words 'Et hec tres unum sunt' ('And these three are One', 1 John 7). He kneels on a red cushion and is clad in armour, covered by a leather jupon emblazoned with the arms of England and France. He wears sword and dagger, golden elbow and knee cops, and golden spurs, and is flanked by two large silver ostrich feathers – his personal badge assumed after the Battle of Crécy – with the motto 'Ich dene' ('I serve') on a scroll below. The poem begins on the next page with an illuminated initial 'O' containing the royal arms, with a border of strapwork and flowers. The text is written on vellum in bastard secretary script (bâtarde), punctuated by small gold initials on coloured grounds. The silver pigment has tarnished badly. L. F. Sandler, in the second volume of her *Gothic Manuscripts, 1285–1385* (London, 1986, p. 177), attributes the work to a group of artists possibly based in late fourteenth-century London, also responsible for the Belknap Hours.

The manuscript belonged to the well-known author, translator and scribe John Shirley (?1366–1456). By 1744 it was in the possession of the Welshman Sir Thomas Mostyn. Sold from Mostyn Hall by Sotheby's in 1920, it was purchased, via Maggs, by the University of London to present to the Prince of Wales (subsequently Edward VIII) when conferring two honorary degrees upon him on 5 May 1921. Edward placed it on permanent loan in the University Library.

1.3

2

Manuscript of William Langland, *Piers Plowman*
Early 15th century
375 × 253 mm; SL.V.17

Among the significant literary manuscripts acquired by Sir Louis Sterling is this handsome copy of William Langland's *Piers Plowman*. This long alliterative poem, part theological allegory, part social satire, exists in over fifty manuscripts but in three different versions, corresponding to progressive revisions of the text by Langland. The present copy contains the latest version, C, produced in the 1380s, followed by two shorter poems, *La Estorie del Evangelie* (in Middle English) and *The Assumption of Our Lady*. It was originally part of a larger compilation written by a single scribe, broken up and sold as three separate manuscripts. The other two are Washington D.C., Folger Library MS V.b.236, containing Robert Mannyng's *Handlyng Synne* (a penitential manual) and *Meditations on the Supper of Our Lord*; and Princeton University Library, MS Taylor 10, containing Mandeville's *Travels*.

Most medieval texts have no title, but here we have the rubric, 'Hic incipit uisio de Petro Ploushman' [*sic*]. The opening is marked by a large blue initial on a decorated gold ground and a bar border composed of gold, rose and blue extending down the page, with gold balls and leaves sprouting from the corners. Divisions within the text are indicated by simple blue initials with red penwork flourishing. The scribe writes in a large, clear hand, with letter forms unusually widely spaced so as to spread out the lines of verse in a volume otherwise designed to be written in double columns.

Evidence for the original owner of a medieval book is usually lacking. However, *ex-libris* inscriptions in several copies and references in medieval wills show that *Piers* was popular with both the clergy and the literate laity. A shield illustrated on the opening page of the Folger MS, the first booklet in the whole volume, bears the arms of Sir William Clopton of Quinton, Gloucestershire, and his wife, Joan Besford, whom he married in 1403. He died in 1419. The volume was probably made for them, probably in London, and the dates make this one of the earliest surviving copies of *Piers Plowman*, produced within a few years of the text's final composition. By the sixteenth century the volume was in the hands of a 'Richard hodgson' and later a 'george langgam'. Sterling attributed subsequent provenance to the antiquary Sir Roger Twysden (1597–1672), but the book dealers W. H. Robinson Ltd bought the volume as a whole in about 1937 from the recusant Giffard family of Chillington Park, Staffordshire.

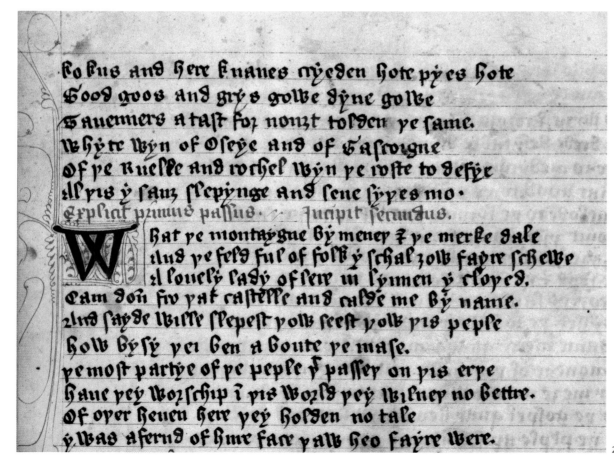

2.1 detail of fol. 4r, with decorated initial

2.2 fol. 1r, with illuminated initial

2.1

In a somur sesoun whan softe was þe sonne
I schop me in to schroudes as y a schepherde were
In abyte as an eremite vnto holy werkes
I wente forþ in þe worlde wondres to here.
And sauz mony selles and selcouthe þynges
And on a maymorwenyng on maluernhulles
Me byfel forto slepe for werynesse of wandryng
And in a launde as y lay lenedy and slepte.
And merueylously y mette as I may zow telle.
Al þe welþe of þys worlde and the wo boþe.
Walkyng as hit were wyterly y sauz hit
Of truþe and of trycheryе treson and gyle
Al y sauz slepyng as y schal zow telle.
Estwarde y behul aftur the sonne
And sauz a toure as y trowede truþe was þer ynne.
Westward y waytede in a whyle aftur.
And sauz a depe dale dey as y leone.
Woned in tho wones and wyckede spyrites
A faur feld ful of folke fond y þer bytwene
Al maner of men þe mene and þe ryche.
Worchyng and wandryng as þe worlde askey.
Summe putten hem to þe plouз and pleyden ful selde
In settyng and sowkynge swonken ful harde.
And wonnen þe wastorus wiþ gloteny destruyen
Summe putten hem to pruyde and paraysden hem þer aftur.
In contenaunce of cloþynge in mony maner wyse
In preyers and penaunces putten hem monyе.
Al for þe loue of oure lord lyueden ful harde
In hope to haue good ende and heuen ryche blys.
As ancres and eremytes þat holdeþ hem in here celles.
Coueyten nat in contreys to caryen aboute.
For no lycorous lyfueloþe here lycame to plese.
And som chesoun chaffare þey cheuesede þe betere.
As hit semeþ to oure syзt þat suche men þryueþ.
And somme muryes to make as mynstrals conney
þat wyllen neyyer swynke ne swete but swere gret oþus·

ESTITVTIO Primo Vtꝗ reſtitutio ſit de neˊ
ceſſitate ſalutis Rñdeo ꝼm Sco.ī quarto di.xv.ar.
.ii.q.iiii §i. in principio ꝙ ſic quia ſicut aufferre
alienum ē peccatum mortale contra ꝑceptū diuinū
negatiuum.ſ. Non ſurtū facies ita & tenere alienū
& ideo ſicut eſt neceſſarium ꝼuare ꝑcepta negatiua
ita neceſſariū ē non tenere alienum inuito domino
& ꝑ conſequens uel actu ſtatim reddere uel ſtatim
uelle reddere cum ſuerit oportunitas unde eſt reſtitutio neceſſaria ut pars
quedā ſatiſſactionis nec generaliter accipiēdo ſatiſſactionē nec ſpecialiter
Generaliter eñi accepta reddit ꝑ peccato equiualens ei in quo peccat̄ non
ſic iſta reſtitutio quia abſꝗ omni redditione ꝑ peccato poſſet reddi ꝑxio
quod ſuun eſt ſicut in mutuis redditur creditori abſꝗ omni ſatiſſactione

3 Franciscus de Platea, *Opus Restitutionum, Usurarum, Excommunicationum*

[Padua?: Printer of Platea, 'Opus Restitutionum'
(H 13034*), not after 1472]; ISTC ip00751000
306 × 209 mm

This text, composed by a professor of law at the
University of Bologna, is perhaps the first work to
cover an economic subject to be printed in the
fifteenth century.

The first section is concerned with restitution, that
is, the need to make full reparation for misdeeds of all
kinds in order to adhere to the seventh Commandment and to attain salvation. The problems covered
range from bribery and overcharging to the kidnap-
ping of nuns, and references are provided to the
literature of canon and civil law in justification of the
penalties prescribed. Business transactions come in
for particular attention. The section on usury follows,
exploring in detail the Church's prohibition on the
taking of interest, together with the types of financial
transaction that can enable risks and profit to be
shared without incurring ecclesiastical censure.
(Some of the methods described have been found to
be relevant to those developing Sharia law today.)
The final section, on excommunication, deals with

the practicalities involved in the penalties by which
offenders against the Church could be deprived of
such Christian rights as access to the sacraments and
to Christian burial.

Neither the place of printing nor the name of the
printer are indicated in the work, but this is one of a
group of four books ascribed on the basis of their
typography to the Veneto region; the survival of copies
today that either are or have been in Paduan libraries
may indicate a Paduan origin. As one of these titles
has a printed date of 1472, and as in addition a copy
of Platea at the Royal Library at The Hague has an
early owner's note dated 1472, we can feel reasonably
confident in attributing the book's date to then.

As was common at the time, large capital letters and
other marks are supplied by hand rather than as part
of the printing process. This hand-finishing is here
represented by handsome penwork in red and blue.

This is the oldest printed book acquired by Herbert
Somerton Foxwell for the Goldsmiths' Library of
Economic Literature. It came to the University of
London in a consignment of twenty-eight cases of
material in 1910, and is the first of the 'works of
exceptional value and interest' from the consignment
to be singled out by the Librarian in a memorandum
to the Library Committee.

3.1 detail of p. 1,
with decorated capital
and penwork

4 St Jerome, *Aureola ex Floribus S. Hieronymi Contexta*

[Rome: Eucharius Silber, *c.* 1482–83]; ISTC ih00159000
206 × 144 mm

The *Aureola ex Floribus S. Hieronymi Contexta* is a monastic rule compiled by Lupus de Oliveto (or Lupo de Olmedo, 1370–1433). Born at Olmedo in the diocese of Avila in Spain, after receiving his education Lupo entered the order of Hieronymites in the Royal Monastery of Our Lady of Guadalupe. With papal consent, in 1424 he introduced a reform in the order establishing the Congregation of the Monk-Hermits of St Jerome of the Observance, or, as they were known in Italy, the Hermits of St Jerome of Lombardy. In 1426 the order obtained a foundation in Rome, which multiplied into seventeen houses in Italy, and in 1429 they adopted a rule of thirty short instructions composed by the founder from the writings of St Jerome.

The Latin text of the monastic rule exists in eight incunable editions, the first printed at Nuremberg in 1470–72. The edition in the Senate House Library was printed in Rome by Eucharius Silber, *c.* 1482–83. It is a small quarto of 53 leaves (lacking the initial blank). Initials are supplied in red ink and capitals are stroked with red. The binding is twentieth-century half-morocco with cloth sides.

The volume comes from the celebrated and remarkable collection of George Dunn (1865–1912), of Woolley Hall, near Maidenhead, and bears his handsome book label printed at the Kelmscott Press in William Morris's 'Golden' type. It was included in Francis Jenkinson's *A List of the Incunabula Collected by George Dunn Arranged to Illustrate the History of Printing* (1923) and was sold, still bound in old boards, in the final part of the Dunn sale at Sotheby's (26 November 1917, lot 3268). It subsequently belonged to the ecclesiastical historian, New Testament scholar and Fellow of Magdalen College, Oxford, Cuthbert H. Turner (1860–1930), with his signature dated 1922, by which time the volume had acquired its present binding. It passed on his death to his godson, the bookman John Carter (1905–1975; signature dated 1930), and the volume carries an unidentified bookplate composed of interlocking initials 'F', 'B' and 'O' in uncertain order.

With the benefit of relative abundance of incunabula in a market still affected by the wartime economy, the University of London bought this volume in 1947 from the London booksellers McLeish and Sons for £12 10*s.* 0*d.*, one of thirty-seven purchases of incunabula made between 1941 and the late 1960s.

4.1 fol. 2r, table of contents

4.2 fol. 3r, beginning of text, with manuscript initial

4.1

4.2

5.1

5

Bernardus de Granollachs, *Lunarium*
ab Anno 1491 ad Annum 1550
[Lyons: Johannes Siber, 1491]; ISTC ig00340700
214 × 148 mm

Johannes Siber began printing at Lyon in 1478 as the partner of Martin Huss, although he had learned his trade at Basel. His speciality as an independent printer, from 1481 onwards, was very large law books – the wear and tear of working the presses at his house caused his landlord to require Siber to give him a copy of every book he printed, on top of the rent. But he also printed a number of texts of medical or more general scientific interest, including several editions of this almanac – either three or four, depending on the correctness of type attributions.

The work of a Barcelona doctor and political figure, Bernat de Granollachs (*c.* 1400–1487), the *Lunarium* was a best-seller in the fifteenth century and beyond. It sets out in annual tables the phases of the moon for each month of the years from 1485 (originally) to 1551,

calculated from the meridian of Barcelona. The dates of forthcoming lunar eclipses are listed, each with its own woodcut showing its extent, and all the movable feasts of the Church. It is a strictly astronomical text, although given a distinct astrological tinge when it was incorporated in the slightly later *Reportorio de los tiempos* by the Spaniard Andrés de Li. Most of the thirty-six extant incunable editions – in Latin (as here), French, Castilian, Italian and the original Catalan – are found in one or two copies, implying that at least as many editions have been destroyed. The present complete copy was long thought to be the unique survivor of its issue, but another, missing the last page of text, was uncovered in the Sorbonne library in Paris in 1995. Like a closely similar Siber printing (GW 11311), with which it shares the setting of some leaves, this edition runs from 1491 to 1550, the years elapsed since the original printing being omitted, and consequently dates from that year or just before.

The book is one of several early almanacs from the collection of Augustus De Morgan.

5.1 fol. d5v–d6r, showing the years 1544–55

6

Heinrich Institoris and Jakob Sprenger,
Malleus Maleficarum
Nuremberg: Anton Koberger, 17 March 1494;
ISTC ii00166000
234 × 170 mm

Books on witchcraft were central to the collecting activity of the psychical researcher Harry Price, whose treasures included Reginald Scot's *Discoverie of Witchcraft* (1584) and James I's *Daemonologie* (1603). Of the eleven copies of the edition of Anton Koberger's 1494 edition of *Malleus Maleficarum* ('Hammer of Witches') recorded in the British Isles, two are from Price's library. They are among nine incunabula in his collection, and the earliest of six editions of the text in his possession. Price hated the book's content, describing it in *The Sphinx* of April 1931 as 'one of the most terrible books known to students of the occult'; Jakob Sprenger he called 'a blood-thirsty German fanatic'.

The *Malleus Maleficarum* was an influential treatise arguing for the existence of witches and trying to educate magistrates on how to detect and convict them. Peter Drach had already printed it three times in Speyer before its issue in Nuremberg by Anton Koberger, owner of southern Germany's largest printing and publishing house. Insofar as Koberger concentrated primarily on religious works, the *Malleus Maleficarum* was a somewhat unusual venture for him. But the work's popularity guaranteed Koberger certain profits, and in that way the text sat well within the astute Koberger's list.

Harry Price acquired this copy of the 1494 Koberger *Malleus Maleficarum* in 1937 for £10 10s. 0d. from the London bookseller Marks. It is bound in late fifteenth- or early sixteenth-century (?)southern German brown calf over wooden boards tooled in blind to a panel design. The edges of the leaves are painted yellow. Both covers are decorated with two concentric four-line frames around all edges, with the lines intersecting at the corners. The central panel is divided vertically by quadruple lines into five compartments. Lozenge-shaped flowerpot tools, large fleurons, round floral tools and round rosette tools decorate the spaces created by the frames and vertical lines. A contemporary manuscript ink title at the top of the upper cover indicates that the book was stored flat, with this upper cover uppermost, shortly after its publication.

The spine is tooled in blind with the title on a later label on the second of the four compartments, a lozenge-shaped flowerpot tool and four round rosette tools on the others, and the date of publication along the foot. Two pairs of clasps hinge at the lower fore-edge and fasten on the upper cover in typically German fashion. These clasps are decorated with 'imitated writing', a technique largely associated with Nuremberg. The lines constituting the decoration are often interpreted as forming the word 'mar[ia]'.

6.1 upper board, with contemporary German blind tooling

6.2 detail of HPB/5A/7, invoice from Marks for *Malleus Malificarum*, 19 February 1937

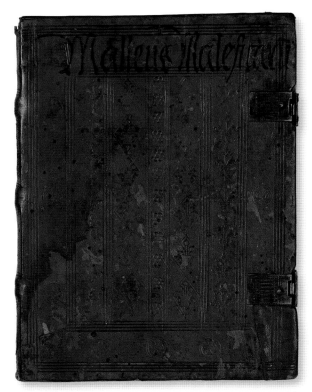

6.1

6.2

7

Geoffrey Chaucer, *The Canterbury Tales*
[London]: Richard Pynson, [between June 1491 and 13 November 1492]; STC 5084; ISTC ic00433000
288 × 201 mm

The early printing of Chaucer's *Canterbury Tales* confirmed the enormous popularity of this work demonstrated by its extensive manuscript circulation. It was the first major title (*c.* 1476) printed by William Caxton, who also produced a second edition in 1483 from a different exemplar or exemplars. Richard Pynson (*c.* 1449–1529/30), a Norman who had begun printing in England in about 1490, produced the third printed edition of Chaucer's *Canterbury Tales c.* 1492. It was later (in 1498) printed by Wynkyn de Worde, making it the only work of Middle English verse to be printed by all three of the major English incunable printers.

Twenty copies of the edition survive (for details see Duff 89). Half of these are imperfect, including the Senate House copy, which has 292 leaves out of a possible 322. Some of these leaves have been inserted from a different copy or copies.

This was very probably the first literary work Pynson printed, and certainly the first of his books to include any woodcuts. He had twenty made for this edition, some of which were used more than once; there are forty-two separate occurrences of these cuts in the Senate House copy. Woodcut illustrations to the *Canterbury Tales* had been first introduced in Caxton's second edition and were henceforward to appear regularly in all subsequent editions of Chaucer's work down to the end of the seventeenth century.

The Senate House copy of Pynson has been decorated by hand: red paraph marks have been added throughout. More unusually, notes in Latin and English and a number of marginal glosses have also been added, in a trained fifteenth-century hand, by someone with access to a manuscript of Chaucer's work which had been carefully compared with this book. The Senate House copy hence provides unusual evidence of the links between manuscript and print cultures in the late fifteenth century in England. A later hand has added further changes to the end of 'The Merchant's Tale' (fol. o vii^r–v).

The subsequent history of the Senate House copy is unclear until it entered the collection of Thomas Grenville (1755–1846), whose arms are stamped on the inside front cover. Grenville also owned two other copies of this edition of Chaucer, one now in the Pierpont Morgan Library, the other of which went to the British Museum (now British Library) with the bulk of his collection. The Sterling copy apparently left Grenville's collection before it was catalogued in 1842 (Payne & Foss, *Bibliotheca Grenvilliana*). It was subsequently in the collection of William Horatio Crawford (1815–1888) and sold for £27 to Quaritch

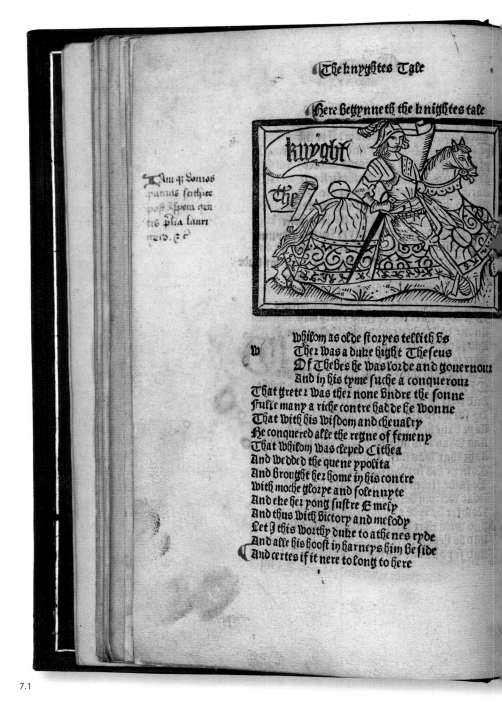

7.1

7.2

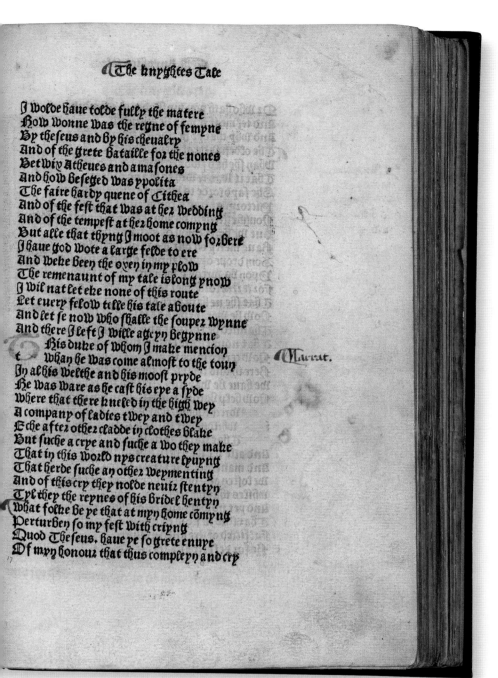

I wolde haue tolde fully the matere
How wonne was the regne of femyne
By thefeus and by his cheualry
And of the grete Bataille for the nones
Betwix Atheues and amafones
And how befeged was ypolita
The faire hardy quene of Cithea
And of the feft that was at her wedding
And of the tempeft at her home comyng
But alle that thyng I moot as now forbere
I haue god wote a large felde to ere
And weke been the oxen in my plow
The remenaunt of my tale islong ynow
I wil nat let eke none of this route
Let euery felow telle his tale aboute
And let fe now who fhalle the fouper wynne
And there I left I wille ageyn begynne
This duke of whom I make mencion
Whan he was come almoft to the toun
In al his welthe and his mooft pryde
He was ware as he caft his eye afyde
Where that there kneled in the high wey
A company of ladies twey and twey
Eche after other cladde in clothes blake
But fuche a crye and fuche a wo they make
That in this world nys creature lyuyng
That herde fuche an other weymenting
And of this cry they nolde neuir ftentyn
Tyl they the reynes of his bridel hentyn
What folke be ye that at myn home comyng
Perturben fo my feft with cryyng
Quod Thefeus. haue ye fo grete enuye
Of myn honour that thus compleyn and cry

Murat.

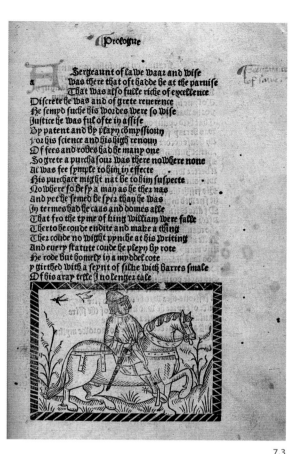

A Sergeaunt of lawe waar and wife
Was there that oft hadde be at the paruife
That was alfo fulle riche of excellence
Difcrete he was and of grete reuerence
He femyd fuche his wordes were fo wife
Juftice he was ful ofte in affife
By patent and by playn commyffioun
For his fcience and his high renoun
Of fees and robes had he many one
So grete a purchafour was there nowhere none
Al was fee fymple to him in effecte
His purchace might nat be to him fufpecte
Nowhere fo befy a man as he ther nas
And yet he femed befyer than he was
In termes had he caas and domes alle
That fro the tyme of king william were falle
Therto he coude endite and make a thing
Ther coude no wight pynche at his writing
And euery ftatute coude he pleyn by rote
He rode but homely in a medlee cote
Y girthed with a feynt of filke with barres fmale
Of his aray telle I no lenger tale

A white cote and a blewe hode wered he
A bagge pype coude he blowe and fowne
And therwith he brought us oute of towne

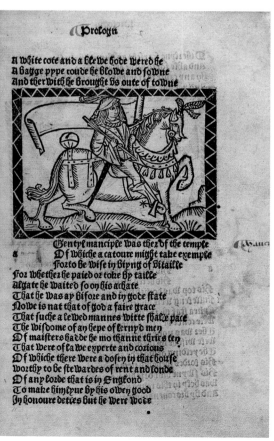

A Gentyl manciple was ther of the temple
Of whiche a catoure might take exemple
For to be wife in byyng of ditaille
For whether he paied or toke by taille
Algate he waited fo on his achate
That he was ay bifore and in gode ftate
Nowe is nat that of god a faire grace
That fuche a lewed mannes witte fhalle pace
The wifdome of an heep of lernyd men
Of maifters hadde he mo thanne thries ten
That were of lawe experte and corious
Of whiche there were a dofen in that houfe
Worthy to be ftewardes of rent and londe
Of any lorde that is in Englond
To make him lyue by his owen good
In honoure detles but he were wode

in his sale on 12 March 1891, lot 699 (it is described there as having 296 leaves). It was later sold at Sotheby's, 19 March 1896, lot 187, *Catalogue of a Portion of the Library of a Collector*, for £200 to 'Stevens'. Sir Louis Sterling bought it in February 1937, also for £200.

7.1 fol. c4v–c5r, *The Knight's Tale*

7.2 detail of fol. m5r, showing manuscript annotations beside *The Man of Law's Tale*

7.3 fol. b1r, Prologue

7.4 fol. b7r, Prologue

8

Gregor Reisch, *Margarita Philosophica*
Strasbourg: Johann Schott, 1504
224 × 156 mm

The *Margarita Philosophica*, or 'Philosophic Pearl', by Gregor Reisch (*c.* 1470–1525), is an encyclopaedic handbook in the form of a dialogue between a pupil (*discipulus*) and a teacher (*magister*), which essentially covers the curriculum of the arts faculty. Reisch had completed the main part of the work before 1496, while himself teaching at the University of Freiburg. It was initially prepared for printing by Johann Amerbach and then published by Johann Schott in Freiburg in July 1503, when Reisch had already become prior of the Freiburg charterhouse.

The second authorised edition, published by Schott in March 1504, is witness to the work's instant success and the complexities of its publication history. Issued merely eight months after the first edition, it alludes to yet another, unauthorised, edition, published by Johann Grüninger in Strasbourg in February 1504. Schott's 1504 edition is particularly notable with regard to illustrations and liminary texts. Even more woodcuts have been added to the already rich array of the first edition. Among them are the full-page image *Typus geometrie* introducing the sixth book on geometry, and an image of Freiburg heading the chapter on rain in the ninth book 'on the origin of natural things'. The 1504 edition has also grown to include more poems praising the work and its author. They are indicative of Reisch's close contacts with well-known humanists, and of their regard for a work that was, in many respects, deeply rooted in the medieval tradition. In the title of one of the new poems, composed by Jakob Locher (*Philomusus*), the *Margarita Philosophica* is described as a 'Cyilopedia' (corrected to 'cyclopedia' in Schott's next edition, of 1508). This is one of the earliest recorded uses of the word 'cyclopaedia' or 'encyclopaedia', which had been coined by Italian humanists at the end of the fifteenth century.

The present copy, which has hand-coloured illustrations and a few annotations in a sixteenth-century hand, is the earliest printed book but one to have come to the University of London through the bequest of Vice-Chancellor George Grote in 1871, one of some sixty sixteenth-century books in his possession. We do not know how Grote had acquired this volume, but an indication of the book's early provenance is the tooling of its sixteenth-century binding, which can be attributed to the 'Blütenrolle' workshop, active in Würzburg until *c.* 1527.

8.1 detail of fol. 2d6v, Freiburg im Breisgau (Germany) in the rain

8.2 title-page

8.3 (overleaf) fol. π2v, 'Typus gramatice'

8.4 (overleaf) fol. p6v, 'Geometria'

8.1

Margarita Philosophica.

L. Balbus.

8.2

Typus geometrie

Jugera

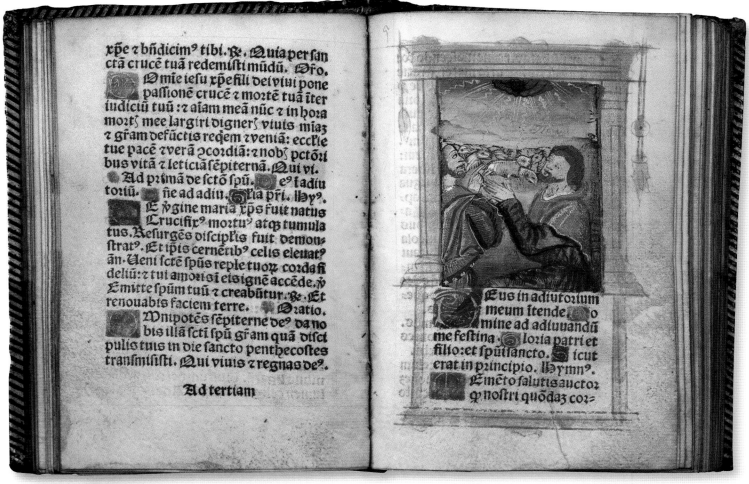

9.1

9 Heures a l'Usaige de Rome Tout au Long sans Riens Requerir
Paris: Germain Hardouyn, [*c.* 1516]
110 × 72 mm

Books of hours, which contain prayers and texts to support devotions thought vital for salvation, had been produced in bulk as manuscripts. They appeared in print after 1470, but production soared after Paris publishers in the mid-1480s invented versions where printed text was accompanied by densely printed illustration and ornament.

As the colophon of this book states, it was printed in Paris for Germain Hardouyn. Gilles Hardouyn was described as a *libraire* in 1494 (see Archives nationales, S 5082/3, fol.192; cited in Renouard, *Répertoire des Imprimeurs Parisiens* (Paris, 1965)). The family were prominent members of the Paris book trade, both Gilles and his brother Guillaume being *libraires-jurés* of the university in the early sixteenth century. An ancestor, Jean Hardouyn, had been a carpenter, and it may be that the Hardouyn family moved into the

capital-intensive publishing business at a time when traditional manuscript book producers found it difficult to survive.

The earliest known Hardouyn book of hours was printed for Gilles in 1498. Around 1504–05, a series of such books in varying formats (sixteenmo, octavo and quarto) was printed for Germain and Gilles Hardouyn by Guillaume Anabat and Antoine Chappiel. By the 1520s, Gilles was himself a printer. Among the books of hours produced by the Hardouyns were a series with images and ornament illuminated by hand. The similarity of the illumination indicates that it was done at the time of manufacture, before the works were dispersed into the book trade. One member of the family, also called Germain, was described as an illuminator and said to be 'most skilled in the art of pictures for writing', suggesting a definite publishing strategy on the part of the Hardouyns to sell printed books ready illuminated. The illustrations follow the standard cycle of images for books of hours.

The book is datable only by the almanach on folio A.i verso, which runs from 1516 to 1537. The colophon

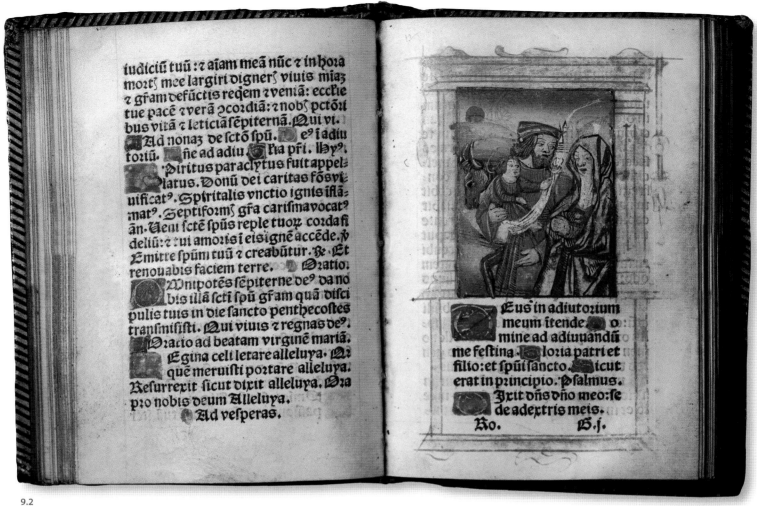

9.2

9.3

gives Germain Hardouyn's address ('between the two doors of the [king's] palace [on the Île de France] at the sign of St Margaret'). The title-page, however, has an illuminated image of a woman playing the lute rather than the device of the Hardouyns, perhaps indicating that it was sold by another bookseller. The images are rapidly but skilfully executed, the compositions and style found in a number of other Hardouyn imprints of this period.

The book was given to the London Institution in February 1836 by Joseph Thomas Hand, a proprietor.

9.1 fol. E7v–E8r, The Annunciation to the Shepherds, for Terce

9.2 fol. F8v–G1r, The Flight to Egypt, for Vespers

9.3 detail of title-page, woman playing a lute

Ihesus. The Floure of the Commaundementes of God
London: Wynkyn de Worde, 1521; STC 23877
279 × 193 mm

This second printing by Wynkyn de Worde of *The Floure of the Commaundementes of God* was, according to its colophon, completed on 8 October 1521; de Worde had produced an earlier edition on 14 September 1510. Both issues describe the work as 'lately translated out of frensshe', but the second edition is the first to identify the translator, which it does by means of a new woodcut added to the final page containing a coat of arms and a depiction of a cart or chariot labelled 'Chertesey'. This is presumably the Andrew Chertsey who lived in London in the parish of St Clement Dane (*fl.* 1508–1532) and produced four other translations of French works of religious instruction for de Worde's press (STC 792, 5198–9, 13685.5–6 and 14558).

Printed editions of a substantial French work called *La Fleur des Commandemens de Dieu* are recorded from the 1490s until at least the 1540s, some from the Paris press of Antoine Vérard. Although it is not clear which French edition Chertsey used, it is likely that his translation is a close one. It is mainly in prose, but uses verse periodically for emphasis, opening with a verse prologue which declares Chertsey's aim of helping readers to escape 'the engine / Of the devyl of hel'. The work as a whole is in two parts, the first listing and analysing the Ten Commandments, the second offering short *exempla* about the results of following or neglecting them. The stories in this part include one about a woman who chose to go dancing instead of listening to a sermon, and was visited in her sleep the following evening by a terrifying vision of devils (fol. clxii); at the other extreme is a story intended to exemplify the Eucharist about 'how the hony bees made vnto Jesu cryste a chapel and an auter', a skilful work blessed by God and praised by men (fol. ccxxii).

Both this edition and the earlier one have a prefatory 'Tabula' or index, several woodcuts and such reader-aids as foliation and individually lettered sections. The Library bought the volume in 1951 for 20 guineas from Mrs Ethel M. Wood, attracted by the desire to own an imprint by one of the three major early English printers (none of whose works it held at the time); it had already noted the item, despite imperfections, as one of the best in her collection. Wood had purchased it at a Sotheby's sale on 14 December 1937 for £18, probably motivated more by piety than bibliophily.

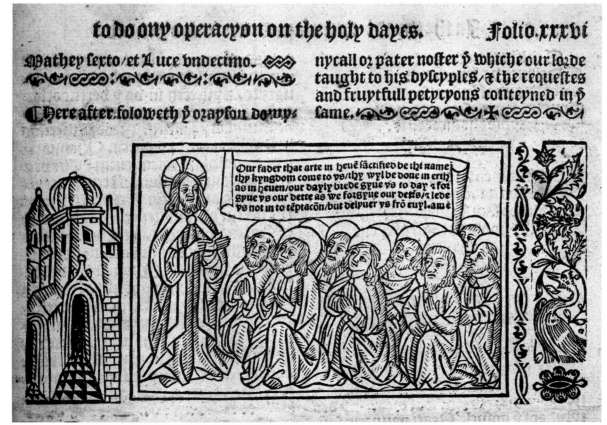

10.1

Here begynneth þ examplayre of the commaundementes of god.   ii.

Lmyghty god the fader / the sone and the holy goost / the whiche is but one onely god i trynyte / pleaseth it þ to enlumyne the hartes and thoughtes of all those þ whiche shall studye this boke the whiche is called þ exemplayre of the commaundementes of god / for it is all of exāples. The whiche examples hath be extracted & gadered in many bokes / in lykewyse as bereth wytnes euery exemple. And hath be transmuted and chaun=
The. ⁂.

ged fyrste frome latyn in to Frensshe / and from Frensshe nowe lately in to Englys=
she tongue. To þ ende þ the symple peo=
ple þ whiche knowe no latyn them may vnderstande. And yf ony saye that there are of examples þ whiche ne bē holy scry=
ptures I cõfesse it well. But I saye that they ben vysyons or myracles that some persones credybles hathe sene ryally / or knowen by experyence þ whiche hath be put in wrytynge. For as moche as they haue cõsonaūce to approue þ holy scryp=
tures.&c. And for that that many exam=
ples ben put in þ boke of the dyscyple it is not for to alegge it as holy persone / or holy scrypture / but for that / þ it was a greate clerke the whiche founde the sayd examples in bokes the whiche we haue
y.i.

Henricus Glareanus, *Dodekachordon*
Basel: Heinrich Petri, 1547; Adams G765
313 × 197 mm

The major influences on the text of the *Dodekachordon*, written by the Swiss humanist Heinrich Glarean (a member of the Erasmus circle in Basel), are the work of two earlier music theorists, Gaffurius and, above all, Boethius. Their treatises provide the material on which the first, more conventional, part of the *Dodekachordon* is based. Glarean also made use of Sebastian Heyden's *Musicae*, and the *Tetrachordum Musices* by Johannes Cochlaeus, as the sources for some of his music examples. Most of the writing seems to have been done in the 1530s; a letter to a fellow musician, Johannes Aal, written in 1538, reveals that the whole of the first and second books were then finished, and that the third merely lacked a handful of polyphonic *exempla*. The treatise was eventually printed, not without

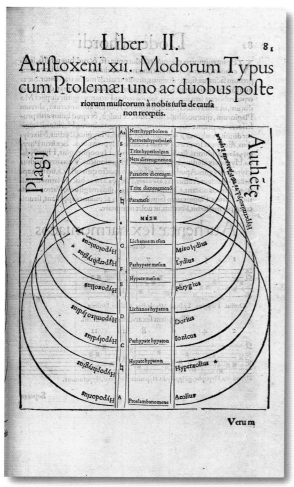

11.1

11.2

considerable difficulty on account of its technical complexity, by Heinrich Petri in Basle in 1549. The Senate House copy is not among the dozens recorded in published bibliographies.

Together with Gioseffo Zarlino's *Le Istituzioni Harmoniche*, published in Venice in 1558, the *Dodekachordon* is one of the two most significant sixteenth-century music treatises, principally on account of its expansion of the modal system. In terms of both its length and typographical elaboration, it is also an impressive example of German Renaissance book production. A large folio volume of some 470 pages, it includes more than 200 music examples and diagrams spread fairly evenly throughout its structure. From the technical point of view the earlier gatherings were the most complicated to print, since in addition to the notated examples these also include tables, diagrams and woodcut illustrations of instruments. The title-page, with its hierarchical arrangement of typefaces, use of both Latin and Greek, and abbreviated references to Classical sources, proclaims the authority and humanist credentials of the author in a visually arresting and effective manner.

The Senate House copy was previously in the library of the British Museum (which sold it as a duplicate in 1831), before passing to the collections of the bibliophile Richard Heber (sold in 1836) and the important French musicologist Charles-Edmond-Henri de Coussemaker (1805–1876), whose library contained more than 1,500 books and manuscripts. Acquired by the Carnegie Trust at the sale of the important library of German and Italian music treatises formed by Alfred Henry Littleton, it was then housed in the College of Preceptors until its presentation in 1932 to the University.

11.1 p. 81

11.2 pp. 36–7

12 Sigmund von Herberstein, *Comentari della Moscovia*
Venice: Giovanni Battista Pederzano, 1550
197 × 150 mm

In 1549 in Vienna the renowned Austrian diplomat and scholar Freiherr Sigmund von Herberstein (1486–1566), veteran of no fewer than sixty-nine diplomatic missions, published his *Rerum Moscoviticarum Commentarii*, the detailed account of two embassies he had undertaken to the Muscovy of Grand Duke Vasilii III, in 1517–18 on behalf of the Emperor Maximilian I, and in 1526–27 for Archduke Ferdinand I.

Priding himself on his knowledge of languages, which included Russian, and on a method of gathering information based on personal observation, probing conversations and careful scrutiny of documentary sources, Herberstein offered sixteenth-century Europe a wide-ranging survey and commentary on what in later books would be called 'the present and past state' of Muscovy or Russia. He provided information on the geography, the governance, the people, their customs and their religion with a degree of persuasive accuracy that brought his book best-seller status and made it widely influential in shaping subsequent views of the country. Herberstein's work was not only one of the earliest examples of travel writing on Muscovy but became the virtually uncontested source of information, acknowledged and unacknowledged, for almost all subsequent writers into the seventeenth century. Prominent among these was the Cambridge scholar and English ambassador Giles Fletcher (1549–1611), who in his own widely acclaimed *Of the Russe Common Wealth* (1591) developed the Austrian's negative appraisal of Muscovy's ruler into a broadside against Russian tyranny and despotism.

Written originally in Latin, his book soon appeared in Herberstein's own German version and in numerous editions and translations down the century and beyond. One of the earliest translations was into Italian, published in Venice in 1550. It is a copy of this edition that was acquired by Professor Matthew Smith Anderson as his last purchase before his death in 2006 and a fitting addition to his incomparable collection of Rossica, which already included a Latin folio edition of the work printed by Joannes Oporinus in Basel in 1551. There was no full English translation until the middle of the nineteenth century, only excerpts that appeared in 1577, but the Latin version was well known, as is evident from lines in 'To Parker', an epistle by the Elizabethan poet George Turbervile, who visited Russia in 1568 with the embassy of Thomas Randolph:

Adieu, friend Parker, if thou list, to know the Russes well,
To Sigismundus book repaire, who all the trueth can tell.
For he long earst in message went unto the savage King,
Sent by the Pole, and true report in each respect did bring.

12.1

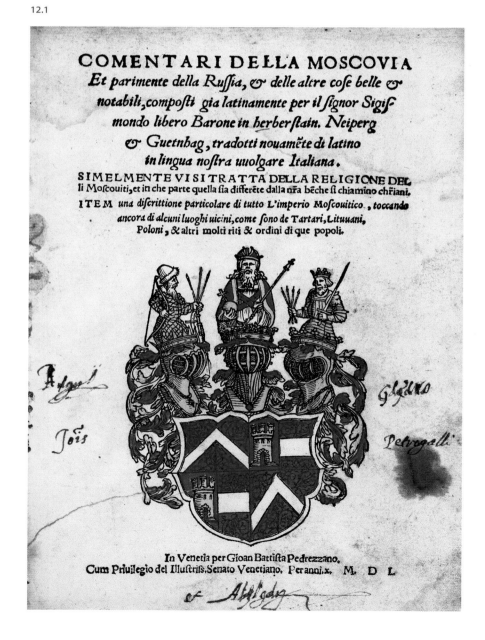

12.1 title-page, with
hand-coloured coat of arms

12.2 fol. 92v

12.3 fol. 93v

12.4 fol. 94r

12.5 fol. 94v

12.2

12.3

12.4

12.5

13 Panoramic drawing of the funeral procession of Anne of Cleves

3 August 1557
Scroll 152 × 1,562 mm; MS817/2/29

Amplissimo hoc apparatus et pulchro ordine proceditur ad funus Anne Clivensiu(m) ducis filie: anno salutis humane die iii(i) Aug [added] *1557*

The funeral of Anne of Cleves and her burial at Westminster Abbey prove the remarkable success of King Henry VIII's rejected fourth queen. Even though the marriage was annulled after only six months and she briefly feared for her life, for the next seventeen years she negotiated a quiet life away from royal politics, honoured with the title 'the King's beloved sister'. She was held in warm regard by Henry's three children and was a good companion to the short-lived Kathryn Howard, who directly supplanted her as Queen.

By the time of her death at Chelsea Manor on 16 July 1557, the throne had passed to Mary Tudor, and

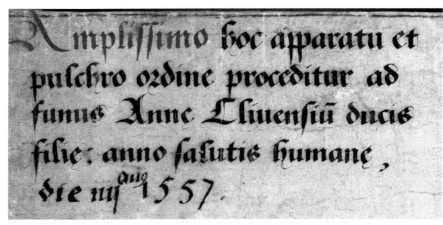

13.1

Roman Catholic rites had been re-established. Anne of Cleves obediently embraced Catholicism, and her funeral, as commanded by Queen Mary, was celebrated using the Catholic rite, led by Edmund Bonner, Bishop of London, and Abbot Feckenham,

13.2

who had re-established the Benedictine monastery at Westminster.

Anne of Cleves is the only one of Henry's wives to lie in Westminster Abbey. Her story is evoked by the panorama of her funeral procession, a skilled though sketchy contemporary drawing dated by the prefatory inscription to 3 (or 4) August 1557 (the fourth 'i' appears as a correction to the original, as does the added 'Aug'), presented on a roll of heavy parchment-coloured paper 152 mm high and 1,562 mm wide, mounted in a box on a double roller. Turning the handles animates the procession: three rows of carefully ordered participants, each individually characterised, some lively, some solemn, some noisy, some quiet. With the boy choristers come the marshals, the candle and torchbearers, the monks of Westminster, the mounted heralds in their elaborate tabards, four mounted and fully draped horses towing the bier, the coffin covered with a cloth bearing a simple cross, accompanied by a prayerful figure at both the foot and the head. Heraldic panels surmount the pall, with Anne's own badge prominently displayed, together with the lion rampant and other royal shields. Accompanying the bier, four mounted heralds in armorial tabards hold high religious banners. The Catholic imagery is clear: two depicting female saints, two more with St George slaying the Dragon and a representation of the Trinity – the crucified Christ held by the enthroned Father.

The 'horse of state', its elaborate gold saddle left empty, follows the bier, and afterwards comes Elizabeth Paulet, Marchioness of Winchester, Chief Mourner, riding side-saddle on her comfortable-looking horse. The Chamberlayne rides near by, with the many assistant mourners, riding side-saddle. Their assistants follow with 'white launes on their heddes'. Members of the household of Anne of Cleves bring up the rear of the procession – a rather unruly bunch jostling for position, flanked by those more solemnly carrying long rosaries in their hands.

Among the many Tudor manuscripts to survive, the many proclamations, property documents, prayer

13.1 title rubric: *Amplissimo*, with a label which identifies the scroll as showing the funeral procession of Anne of Cleves

13.2 the funeral bier identified through heraldry, accompanied by mounted heralds carrying religious banners and followed by the chief mourners, led by the Marchioness of Winchester and her ladies, riding side-saddle

13.3

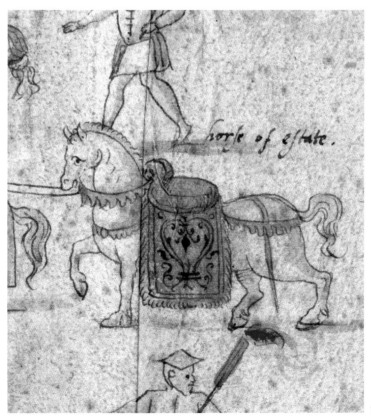

horse of estate.

13.4

13.5

13.3 the community of Westminster Abbey bearing the candles and the triple processional crosses

13.4 the unmounted 'horse of estate' following the bier

13.5 the household of Anne of Cleves, mounted and on foot, bring up the rear of the procession

books, painted portraits and miniatures, this fine roll shows the quality of draftsmanship of this unknown artist. This roll bears witness to the importance of the funeral procession in Tudor England. Its significance in its own day is suggested through a copy, larger in format, its character and detail diminished, preserved in an early seventeenth-century manuscript (British Library MS Additional 35324) which also includes copies of funeral processions of other Tudor figures, including Mary, Queen of Scots, and Queen Elizabeth I. Full of energy and life, this documentary reading provides direct evidence of the event. Despite there being no attempt at portraiture, the costume and the order within the procession provide identification of each of the groups. Some of the key figures are named in captions written in a small cursive hand. The perfect order, the atmosphere, the energy of the figures and the head-tossing horses not only bring to life the sounds, action and detail of this spectacular London event but also create a dynamic sense of its significance – the funeral of the last surviving of the old King's wives.

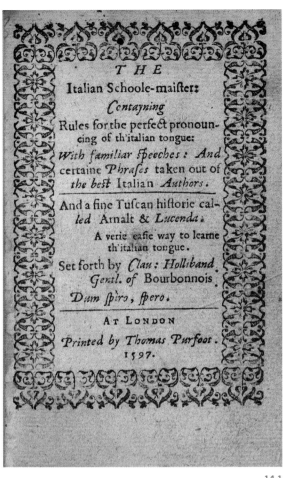

14.1

14.1 title-page

14.2 detail of fol. D4r, showing 'scurrilous' text

14

Claudius Hollyband, *The Italian Schoole-Maister: Contayning Rules for the Perfect Pronouncing of th'Italian Tongue*
London: Printed by Thomas Purfoot, 1597 (first state); STC 6759
140 × 88 mm

The explosion of literacy and trade in the late sixteenth century created opportunities for immigrants such as Claude Hollyband, who taught foreign languages – chiefly French and Italian – to England's rising merchant class through his phrasebooks, and to their children in his school.

A native of Moulins (he styles himself '*gentilhomme bourbonnais*'), Claude Desainliens and his fellow Huguenots dispersed from that Protestant stronghold around 1565, ahead of the St Bartholomew's Day massacre. By 1568 he had, like many Huguenots, Anglicised his name, to Claudius Hollyband, or Holiband. For a while he kept a school in Lewisham, at the time a small village south of London, but for the most part he taught in St Paul's Churchyard, by the signs of the Lucrece and subsequently the Golden Ball.

Hollyband's texts consist of dialogues from everyday settings in columns of Italian or French, placed adjacent to their English equivalents (like modern phrasebooks). They are vivid windows on daily life in Elizabeth's England. Into many dialogues he injects real places and people, and other autobiographical touches. In a 'familiar talke' entitled 'Of the Notarie or Scriuener', created for Hollyband's Italian-language primer, we are in St Paul's Churchyard, a principal haunt for these tradesmen. Not coincidentally, we are also near Hollyband's school (he does not shy away from self-advertisement). After some colourful comments about an M. N., 'a rich vilaine, without *Learning, Ciuilitie, Humanitie, Courtesie*, whose face sheweth that he is alwaies shiting' (see below), we meet a 'jewel among scriveners', 'verie well learned […] but aboue all, an honest man, and good bringing vp': Richard Collins, Clerk of the Stationers' Company, who must have done Hollyband some good turn.

This version of the dialogue was apparently disallowed by the authorities: in most surviving copies the colloquy has been rewritten to omit the remarks about M. N., and Collins is not named. The narrator in another dialogue is going to court on a money matter and shares with his interlocutor a dim view of the officers, such as serjeants-at-arms, who are involved in the judicial process.

Behold, there be three or foure, and more then of flies
and like vermine: for you know that Watermen, Porters,
*   & Sergeants, are the dragges of the earth.*
Of curtesie sir, cast me not into the hands of such
*   devilish knaues.*

The revised printing plays a different tune:

Behold, there be three or foure: but it is needelesse to
*   call them, for the good man will agree with you.*

The printer, having produced a whole run, had to print two new gatherings to replace the offending originals, but the Senate House Library copy escaped the inserted reprints.

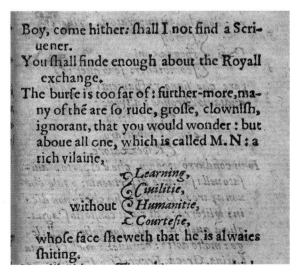

14.2

15 Robert Devereux, 'An Apologie of the Earle of Essex'
17th century
233 × 169 mm; MS287

MS287, 'An Apologie of the Earle of Essex', is a copy of a tract by Robert Devereux, second Earl of Essex (1565–1601), addressed anonymously to Anthony Bacon. The text differs slightly from that of the first printed edition of 1600 (STC 6787.7), which also included a letter from Essex's sister Lady Rich to the Queen on Essex's behalf. The tract, without the letter, was reprinted in 1603 by Richard Bradocke (STC 6788), an edition in which the work is described as having been 'Penned by himself in Anno 1598'.

By 1598 a series of disastrous enterprises had strained Essex's high standing as Queen Elizabeth's favourite. Essex supported the policy of committing more resources to help French and Dutch allies combat the power of Spain. In June 1596 Essex had shared command in the expedition to sack Cádiz, a temporary victory which, however, led to further conflict with the Queen once it transpired that Essex had hidden much of the plunder from her officials.

In August 1597, appointed to lead naval and military forces to attack the Spanish fleet at Ferrol, Essex disobeyed the Queen's instructions and sailed to the Azores, hoping to capture the Spanish silver fleet. Essex failed to achieve either goal and returned home in disgrace. His continued wish for a Spanish war suffered a further set-back when Henry IV of France decided to secure peace with Spain. Essex was increasingly isolated at court, having been accused of preventing England from making peace.

As on other occasions when frustrated at court, Essex appealed to a wider public by writing this impassioned 'Apologie', in which he defended his 'reputation of a most faithfull subject and zealous Patriot' and provided a spirited defence of all his military engagements.

Essex regained the Queen's favour sufficiently to be appointed Lord-Lieutenant of Ireland in 1599, charged with destroying the rebellion led by the Earl of Tyrone. Having instead concluded a peace treaty with Tyrone, he was charged with treason on 20 March 1600. Although he survived that crisis, Essex led an abortive rebellion to unseat the Queen, and he was executed on 25 February 1601.

The manuscript formerly belonged to the distinguished lawyer, judge and one-time Chancellor of the Exchequer Sir Julius Caesar (1558–1636). Sold at auction for 3 shillings in December 1757, it subsequently entered the libraries of Horatio (Horace) Walpole (1717–1797), Sir Thomas Phillipps (1792–1872) and ultimately Sir Edwin Durning-Lawrence (1837–1914).

15.1 detail of p. 3, showing the beginning of the manuscript

15.2 title-page of the 1603 printed edition

15.1

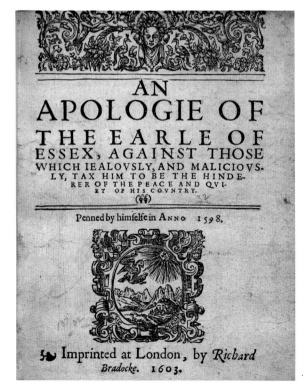

AN
APOLOGIE OF
THE EARLE OF
ESSEX, AGAINST THOSE
WHICH IEALOVSLY, AND MALICIOVS-
LY, TAX HIM TO BE THE HINDE-
RER OF THE PEACE AND QVI-
ET OF HIS COVNTRY.

Penned by himselfe in ANNO 1598.

Imprinted at London, by Richard
Bradocke. 1603.

15.2

16 Gottfried Rabe, *Nohtwendige Antwort und Defensionschrifft der christlichen Revocation Predigt des ehrwirdigen Godefridi Raben*

Wittenberg: Printed by G. Müller, 1602
186 × 149 mm

Gottfried Rabe's *Nohtwendige Antwort* is the penultimate element in a late example of denominational invective that began with the Reformation. Rabe, who is known only through his works, was, as the title of this and his former works states, a former Augustinian monk and preacher in Prague. In 1601 he converted to Protestantism. He was welcomed and adopted as a mouthpiece in the Protestant stronghold of Wittenberg, where 'because he had previously preached Papacy publicly, he himself saw the value and need of revoking it publicly'. Rabe's earlier printed sermons, published in various German towns in 1601, are *Eine christliche Predigt, vom Gebet*, a relatively innocuous sermon on John 16, and *Christliche Revocation Predigt*, which takes as its text Christ as the Good Shepherd (John 16) and combines the message of God's mercy with a thorough and virulent attack on Catholic beliefs and practices. This latter publication attracted at least two rebuttals, from Richard Prumbaum in Mainz and from Theodor Cycneus (i.e.,Valentin Leucht), whose *Kurtzer doch gründtlicher Gegenbericht auff des Gottfried Raaben … Reuocation Predigt* ran into three editions in Frankfurt and Mainz. The *Nohtwendige Antwort* is Rabe's reply to Cycneus. It was itself refuted in Cycneus's *Replica oder Beweißliche Ableinung der Nichtwerdigen Defension Schrifft …* (1602).

At 96 pages, the tract is considerably longer than the average for such works (32 pages). Otherwise, its appearance is typical: a cheap quarto production on brownish paper with show-through, with the predominant vernacular in black letter and Latin text in roman type. Its monologic style is earthy and direct, its tone indignant and abusive. Rabe regards himself as a contemporary David beset by his enemies, and protests against Cycneus's personal vilification. He gives his autobiography and answers Cycneus's calumny (for example, Cycneus's assertion that Rabe's mother had been a goose-girl). He then, predictably, asserts Protestant supremacy, dismisses the Pope as Antichrist, stresses salvation through grace, attacks monks for unchastity and gambling and the vows imposed on them as human decrees, and rebuts various elements of Catholic belief and practice.

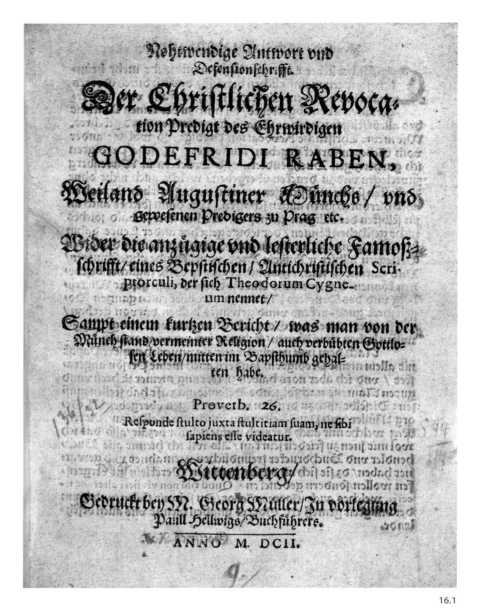

16.1

The circular ink ownership stamp 'Bibl. Bernhard v. Rat.' on the final page proclaims the book to have belonged at some stage to the St Bernhardin church library in Breslau. Sir Edwin Durning-Lawrence, the most recent personal owner of the item, was unaware of its content. He purchased and accessioned it with a clutch of rare Rosicrucian books of similar age, listed it under the heading 'Rosicrucian books' in his manuscript catalogue and shelved it with them. The pamphlet is noteworthy as the only recorded copy in England and one of just two copies in Great Britain.

16.1 title-page

17 [Sebastián de Granadilla?], *Aqui comiença vna obra, vtil y prouechosa para todos, de los Mandamientos. Agora nueuamente hecha, por vn deuoto de Iesu Christo*

Alcalá de Henares: Iuan Gracián, 1607; Palau y Dulcet (2nd edn) 14319 and 108399

189 mm × 143 mm

This anonymous work is attributed, on no clear grounds, to Sebastián de Granadilla of Salamanca, a painter specialising in the decoration of three-dimensional religious works such as funerary monuments and processional images. His only other printed work (also held at Senate House Library), *Coplas del año de mil y quinientos y nouenta y nueue las quales contienen las notables cosas que acontecieron en estos dos años esteriles* (Salamanca: Antonia Ramirez, viuda, 1607), is a verse account of the Salamanca famine of 1598 and 1599. As this type of publication deals in topicality, and as the licence to print is of 1599 and the edition is of 1607, the surviving edition is probably a reprint occasioned by a new famine in 1606.

The Ten Commandments have circulated in popular works of mass religious instruction since the beginning of printing, often included in primers for the teaching of reading. (The present work is aimed at adults, not children.) Small and flimsy, these works were often read to pieces.

The author offers an orthodox exposition of the Decalogue in octosyllabic *coplas reales*. The woodcut of the Crucifixion is broadly in keeping with the Christian theme, but signs of wear suggest it was inherited from earlier works. Like a preacher, the author gives glimpses of the errors he castigates: (2nd Commandment) 'Do not swear by the Faith, or the Cross; it is no longer acceptable to swear by God; nowadays even ten-year olds swear by Our Lady'; (3rd Commandment) 'Instead of going to Mass, people go hunting or play skittles'; (4th Commandment) 'It is better to fight the Moors and read saints' lives'.

The printer Juan Gracián (here described as deceased) printed at the university town of Alcalá de Henares from 1568 to his death in 1587; his widow, María Ramírez, took over his press until 1624. The orthodox Catholic subject matter of the book in hand is typical of a large part of the output of the press. Among the literary productions of the press are the first editions of Cervantes's *La Galatea* (1585) and *Las sergas de Esplandián* (1588), also known as the Fifth Book of *Amadís de Gaula*.

17.1

This is the only copy known to Julián Martín Abad in his 1999 bibliography *La imprenta en Alcalá de Henares (1601–1700)* (item 84), and, indeed, appears to be unique. No other edition is recorded. Both it and the *Coplas* are from the renowned collection of Henry Huth and his son Alfred H. Huth, which was sold by the auctioneers Sotheby, Wilkinson & Hodge over the period 1911–20; such items of popular printing were a Huth interest.

17.1 p. 1, with woodcut of the Crucifixion

18 Petrius Bertius, *Theatrum Geographiae Veteris, Duobus Tomis Distinctum*

Amsterdam: J. Hondius, 1618–19

433 × 285 mm

The century or so following the advent of printing saw the development of increasingly sophisticated and accurate cartography, producing printed maps and atlases to replace the crude approximations of the medieval mind, with maps whose outlines and proportions we can recognise today. Between the late sixteenth and late seventeenth centuries the Low Countries became the centre of excellence for mapmaking, not only because many of the great

cartographers such as Mercator, Ortelius and Blaeu were based there, but also because a number of Dutch publishing houses, particularly in Antwerp and Amsterdam, developed the skills and the market for handsome atlases.

Peter Bertius (1565–1629) belonged to this tradition, beginning his authorial career with a Latin version of a popular small atlas originally published in Dutch (*Caert Thresoor*, 1598), which Bertius translated as *Tabulae Contractae* (1600). A native of Flanders, he became librarian and professor of mathematics at Leiden in 1593 but ended his life in Paris after becoming caught up in the religious controversies of early seventeenth-century Holland. His most celebrated work is this large-scale world atlas based on the text of Ptolemy, the most influential geographer of the ancient world, whose *Geographia* was compiled around AD 150. Bertius's edition includes nearly fifty engraved folding maps of Europe and Asia, drawn from earlier work by Mercator and Ortelius.

Printing technique of the time could produce maps only in black and white, but colouring could be added by hand at extra cost. This copy has all its maps finely coloured, as it immediately entered English royal ownership; the elaborate binding, with the royal arms at the centre of an all-over pattern of thistles and fleurs-de-lys, shows that the book's first owner was either James I (d. 1625) or his son Charles I. Although the binding has suffered both wear and repair over the centuries, it would originally have been very handsome and an example of the best work of the upmarket London binderies of the time.

In 1757 the accumulated book collections of English monarchs passed into the newly founded British Museum and became known as the Old Royal Library. A late eighteenth-century *Museum Britannicum* ink stamp and a (largely erased) shelfmark testify to the book's sojourn in Montague House, the Museum's original home. It did not make the Library's transition in the 1830s to the Museum's current Bloomsbury headquarters; another ink stamp records its disposal as a duplicate from the Museum Library in 1804. It then passed into the library of the London Institution (founded 1806), in whose first printed catalogue, of 1813, it appears (p. 563). The University of London acquired the book upon the Institution's dispersal in 1912, and named it in the Library Committee's annual report for 1925 as one of seventy-six 'items of special interest and value' from that source.

18.1

18.1 upper board, showing royal Stuart arms

18.2 title-page

THEATRI
GEOGRAPHIAE VETERIS
Tomus prior
in quo
CL. PTOL. ALEXANDRINI
Geographiæ libri VIII
Græcé et Latiné
Græca ad codices Palatinos collata
aucta et emendata sunt
Latina infinitis locis corecta
opera
P. BERTII Christianissimi Galli-
arum Regis Cosmographi.

AMSTELODAMI
Ex officinâ Iudoci Hondij
Anno 1618.

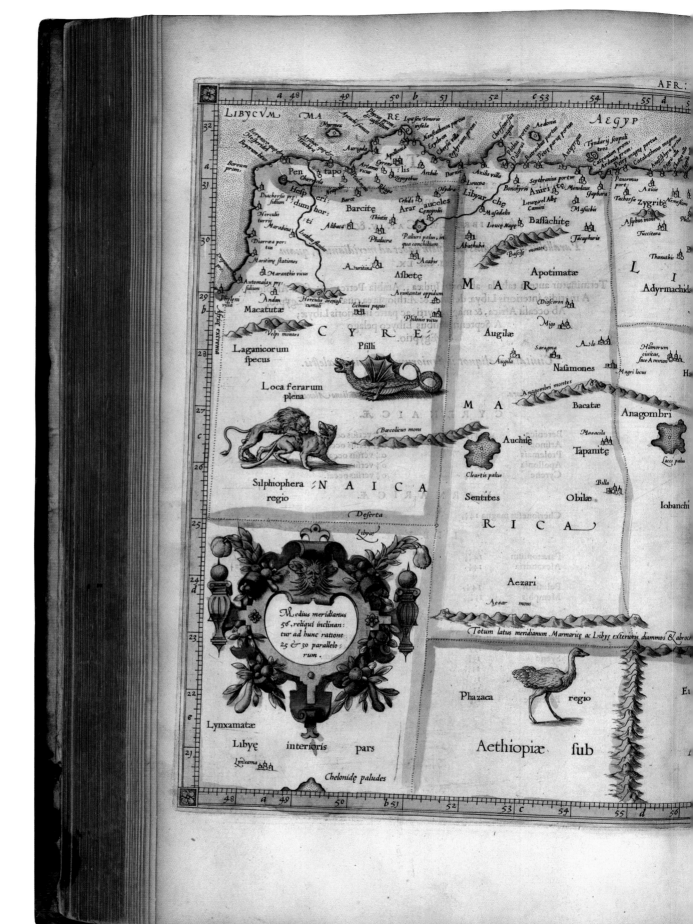

18.3 fol. O1v–O2r, map of Africa

LIBYCVM MA RE AEGYP

Pen tapo lis

Hesp eri dum hor ti

Barcitę

Lilyarche

Baſſachitę

Asbetę

Apotimatę

Adyrmachida

MAR

CYRE

Augilę

Naſamones

Loca ferarum plena

Laganicorum ſpecus

Pſilli

MA CYRENAICA

Anagombri montes

Bacatę

Anagombri

Auchiſę

Tapanitę

Laci palus

Silphiophera regio

NAICA

Cleartis palus

Billa

Sentites

Obilę

Iobanchi

RICA

Deſerta

Libyę

Aezari

Aezar mons

Totum latus meridianum Marmaricę ac Libyę exterioris diammos & abroch

Medius meridianus 56, reliqui inclinan: tur ad hunc ratione 25 & 30 parallelo: rum.

Phazaca regio

Et

Lynxamatę

Libyę interioris pars

Aethiopię ſub

Lynxama

Chelonidę paludes

PELA: GVS

Iudææ pars

Anthedon
Ostracine
Rhinocorura
Iamnitorum portus
Azotus
Ascalon
Gazæorum portus
Raphia
Sirbonis palus
Eluſa

Eboda

Arabię petreę pars

Berzamma
Gubba
Gypſaria
Geraſa
Elana

Heliopolites n.
go inferior

Peluſium
Herculis parua ciuit
Phacuſa
Caſſio

Bubaſtus

Tanis
Hercum
Heliopolis

Aphroditopolis

Babylon

Arabes

Clisma præ
ſidium

Pharan prom.

Memphites n.
Memphis
Acanthon
Arſinoe n.
Arſinoites n.
Ptolemais ſtatio
Heracleo
Aphrodi
Heracliæ magna ci

Aegy

Drepanum prom:

Saſpirene

Oxyryn
chites n.
Hep
no
Cynopoli:

Oxyryncha
Cynopolis

Sinus

Acoris n.
Alabaſtra

Hermopoli:
tis
Hermopolites n.
Phylace
Lycopolites
no.
Hypſele
Hypſelites
no.

Antinoi ciuit
Antinoites

Alabaſtri
nuæ mons

Arabici

Aphro
Aphroditopo:
tes no.
Crocodilorum
ciuit

Antęi
opolites no.

Paſſalus

Miſormus

Ptolemais Her
Thini
my
tes no.
Abydus
Diospolis parua
Diospolites no.

Panopolis

Panopoli:
tes no:

Porphyrites
mons

Philoteras portus

Aius mons

Tentyra
Tentyrites no.
Pampanis
Tathyris

Lepidotum
tes no:

Chenoboscia
Cæne id eſt
noua ciuit

Coptites no:
Coptos
Apollinis parua
ciuit

Leucos id eſt
albus portus

Acabe
mons
Nechefia

Memnon
nomus

Aphroditis id
eſt Veneris
inſula

Hermonthis
Latopolis
Hermonthites
no.

Iouis magna ciuit:
Tuphium
Thebarum nomus
Chnubis
Elethya id eſt Luci:
nę ciuitas

Smaragdus mons

Apollinis ciuit
magna
Phthenthis
mus

Toi
ais

Niger lapis
mons

Lepte extrema

pars

Ombi
Syene

Cataractes minor

Berenice

Pentadactylus
mons

Phylæ
Sacra Sycaminus

Pſelcis
Dodecaschœni
Metacompſo

Baſanitus la:
pis mons

Adęi

Bazium
promont:

Aquathonis
inſula

Colobi

Priocotus
mens

Cataractes maior

Tasitia

Pnups

Chersonesus

Boum
Autoba

Berithis

Troglodi:
cę pars

Phthur
Gerbo

Nilus fluuius

Mnemain prom
Ihus mons
Bathus portus
Dioscorum por:
tius

Pistre
Pateta

Ruadſtæ

Oaſites maior

Oaſſis magna

Tinodes vel arenoſus mons

Libyci montes

RIOR

Libyæ gyptij

Hermonthites

pars

Nitriotę

Oaſites mi:
nor

Oaſitę duę Heptano:
mis aſcribuntur

Solis fons

Mareotis

Ogdęmi

Maſtitæ

Mæruis
lacus

Dionyſia

Oaſſis parua

Chimax

Zyges

Mareo
Proſodite
nom.

Banchis

Scythiaca
regio

Naucratis
Scyathis
Andropo:
lis
Latone

Re:
Nici
Androlis

Memphis

Babylon

Saw
Buſiris

Ogdamus mons

Aſſis mons

Pnigeus

Catabathmus
paruus

Antiphra
villa

Glaucum
Pedonia villa

Iera

Antiphilis
Coby
Paliuria victis

Alexandria
Mercury
paruus

Butos
Cabaſa

Xoes

Saw
Taua

Leonto:
palis

Phamothis

Laodamantii

Phoenus portus

Leucoſtæ luus

Thmuis
Selennytus

Panephyſos

Metelis

Phamothis

Maſtitæ

Y A

X

19 *Mr William Shakespeares Comedies, Histories, & Tragedies: Published According to the True Original Copies*

London: Printed by T. Cotes for W. Aspley, 1632;
STC 22274b
339 × 230 mm

Sir Edwin Durning-Lawrence acquired his Shakespeare Second Folio in May 1894 from the antiquarian bookseller Henry Sotheran for £22, including commission. The following month he bought the Fourth Folio for £22 10s. 0d., and two years later the Third for £60. He had already acquired a copy of the First Folio for £115.

The Second Folio was published nine years after the First, when all copies printed (around 750 in number) are assumed to have sold out. The content is the same, except for three new elegies added to the preliminary pages, but the texts of the plays contain about 1,700 variants. Many are insignificant, consisting of new typographical errors and modernised spelling and punctuation. At one time the Second Folio was regarded mainly as a page-by-page reprint of the First. But now the work of the revisers is becoming increasingly valued; in many instances they corrected errors and corruptions, rectified stage directions and supplied missing words. In particular, they corrected errors due to misunderstandings of foreign languages, for instance improving a passage in Latin in *Love's Labour's Lost* and the French-language scenes in *Henry V*. Iconic as the First Folio is, about 230 copies of that – a good proportion – are now extant, rendering the Second Folio, with under 100 recorded copies, the rarer book.

Although Durning-Lawrence bought his Shakespeare Folios at a time when it was becoming the thing for serious book collectors to acquire them as a set, his primary purpose in purchasing them was to prove his theories about the Baconian authorship of Shakespeare's works, and in this respect the Second Folio was more important to him than the others. His copy was one of the rare issues, printed by Thomas Cotes for William Aspley, containing a textual variant in Milton's Epitaph on Shakespeare, a poem appearing for the first time in the Second Folio, which he regarded as a highly significant clue to Bacon's authorship. For the usual reading in line 4, 'star-ypointing pyramid' (glossed as 'pyramid pointing to the stars'), Durning-Lawrence's copy has 'star-ypointed pyramid', which he argues refers to a pyramid with a star on its apex, that is, a beacon (pronounced 'bacon'). A facsimile of the page containing this epitaph is inserted at the back of this copy, presumably made for use at lectures. The page itself is attached to a stub on different paper, apparently inserted from another copy. Durning-Lawrence believed that copies of the Second Folio containing this page had been issued 'only to those to whom Bacon's secrets had been entrusted' (Edwin Durning-Lawrence, *Key to Milton's Epitaph on Shakespeare* ([London], 1914), p. 6).

19.1

19.1 fol. A5r, preliminary leaf
with poem by John Milton

19.2 title-page

7

MR WILLIAM
SHAKESPEARES
COMEDIES,
HISTORIES, and
TRAGEDIES.

Published according to the true Originall Copies.

The second Impression.

Martin Droeshout sculpsit London.

LONDON,

Printed by *Tho. Cotes*, for *William Aspley*, and are to be sold at the signe
of the Parrat in Pauls Church-yard. 1 6 3 2.

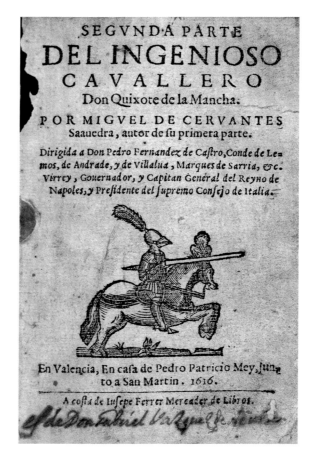

20.1

20.2

 20 **Miguel de Cervantes Saavedra, *El Ingenioso Hidalgo Don Qvixote de la Mancha***
Valencia: P. P. Mey for J. Ferrer, 1605–16
148 × 99 mm

The original form (what we now call Part I) of Cervantes's popular comic romance parodying chivalry books first appeared in Madrid in late 1604 (dated 1605). It was an immediate success but full of errors, and the same Madrid publisher brought out a further, hastily revised, edition by the spring of 1605. Two editions in Lisbon (at the time under Spanish rule) followed in the same year, based on the first edition of 1604 with all its errata, and then another in Valencia that used the second Madrid edition for its text. This is the one held by the Library.

It was ten years before Cervantes, during the incredibly productive final years of his life, completed a Part II, no doubt spurred on by the appearance in 1614 of a continuation of his novel by someone writing under the name of Alonso Fernández de Avellaneda. In his own Part II, Cervantes brilliantly turns this potential disaster to his advantage by incorporating one of the principal characters of the bogus Part II into his own narrative: this personnage, on meeting the real knight and his squire in the flesh, signs an affidavit to

the effect that he now has no doubt that the characters with whom he had associated in Avellaneda's work were complete impostors.

Again the volume was published in Madrid. Meanwhile, another four editions of Part I had come out in Milan, Brussels and Madrid (nine editions in all in the space of the ten years to 1615). There are four printings of Part II outside Madrid. The Valencia edition, held by the Library, is the first of them, and is considered to be the most carefully typeset of all five, although it suffered slightly more censure at the hands of the Inquistion. Sales of these early editions of Part II were relatively modest.

Both the volumes held by the Library are rare in the UK, especially the 1616. They had been among fifty-eight editions of Don Quixote owned by the Paris-based Spanish book-lover Juan González Asúnsolo before Edith, Lady Durning-Lawrence (1844–1929), purchased them for £60 from the London antiquarian booksellers Davis & Orioli in December 1923. They then joined a smaller number of Cervantine items acquired by Edith's husband, Sir Edwin Durning-Lawrence – who in 1897 had also purchased Thomas Shelton's English translation of the work (1612–20) for a staggering £116 12*s*. 0*d*. – in the belief that the work in fact stemmed from Sir Francis Bacon.

20.1 spines of both volumes

20.2 title-page, vol. 2

20.3 another edition of Don Quixote from the Durning-Lawrence Library: Cervantes, *Histoire de l'admirable Don Quichotte de la manche*, 3rd edn (Paris, 1695), vol. 1, picture facing p. 93, showing Don Quixote's adventure with the windmills

21 Thomas Peedle and Thomas Cozbie, *The Falacie of the Great Water-Drinker Discovered*
[London]: Printed by B. Alsop for T. Dunster, 1650; Wing (2nd edn) P1052
184 × 136 mm

This slight tract perfectly epitomises the weird and wonderful output of London's printing presses during the seventeenth century, which fascinated and appalled contemporaries and which have intrigued scholars and collectors ever since. One such enthusiast was the sometime conjuror and psychic researcher Harry Price, who in the short-title catalogue of his collection described this work as 'exceptionally rare', and in an exhibition catalogue of 1934 called it a 'rare and curious book on regurtitation'.

The pamphlet is indeed scarce (there are four other known copies in public libraries), and it is undoubtedly curious. It tells the tale of Floram Marchand, the 'grand boyeur' of Tours, who claimed to be able to 'turn water into wine', whose stage act involved vomiting liquids with the 'tincture, strength and smell' of various wines and beers, and who could project 'three pipes' simultaneously to a distance of 'four or five yards'. It is this striking feat that is depicted on the pamphlet's dramatic woodcut. The purpose of this tract, however, was to expose rather than to celebrate Marchand, and to 'undeceive' readers who had been 'amazed at the wonder but could not discover the secret'. Its authors, the very entrepreneurs who had brought Marchand to England, denounced him as an impostor, whose deceit had been connived at by Cardinal Mazarin and who had grasped the opportunity to become 'famous' in England, where his 'moist cheat' was 'never heard of'. Disillusioned with their prize exhibit, Peedle and Cozbie demonstrated that the show involved not magic but trickery, involving a carefully purged stomach and the swallowing of strange pills and vast quantities of water, as well as the use of glasses tainted with vinegar. The result was a bizarre tale, but one that was far from out of place in seventeenth-century England. It makes sense in a world where monstrous births and mysterious wonders filled impromptu stages and exhibitions, as well as the pages of crude pamphlets. It also makes sense as part of a broader culture of curiosity and enquiry which accompanied the scientific revolution. And it epitomised perfectly the developing culture of cheap print. It was in essence a crude advertisement – Peedle and Cozbie explained that they would be available to make 'experimental proof' of their claims 'at widow Gilman's House in Golden Lane, next to the sign of the Peel' – and its publisher was an early literary inhabitant of Grub Street, a location just beginning to become associated with cheap and scurrilous pamphlets. That said, the authors' claim that the tract had been 'licenced' by the republican authorities was indeed true, and the pamphlet was entered in the Stationers' Register on 21 June 1650, three days before it appeared in London's bookshops.

21.1

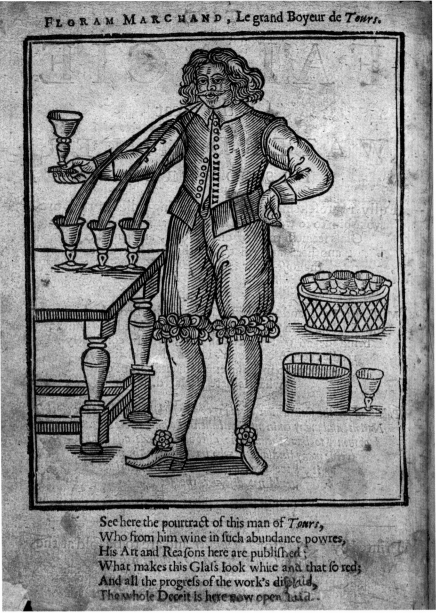

FLORAM MARCHAND, Le grand Boyeur de *Tours*.

See here the pourtract of this man of *Tours*,
Who from him wine in such abundance powres,
His Art and Reasons here are published;
What makes this Glass look white and that so red;
And all the progress of the work's displaid,
The whole Deceit is here now open laid.

21.2

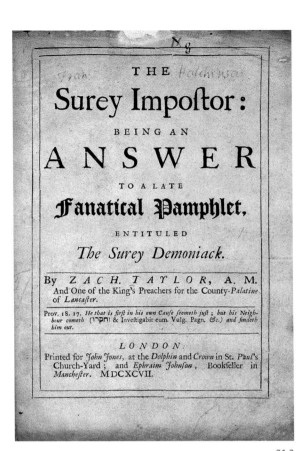

21.3

The Surey Impostor.

THE Reader is desired to take Notice, That (through the Carelessness of the Cutter) the Hand in Sir *Edmund Ashton*'s Coat of Arms, mention'd *p.* 17. is left out.

21.4

21.1 frontispiece

21.2 fol. A1v, showing woodcut of Floram Marchand

21.3 an example of another pamphlet concerning fraud from the Harry Price Library of Magical Literature: Zachary Taylor, *The Surey Impostor* (London, 1697), title-page

21.4 *The Surey Impostor*, frontispiece

**Robert Stileman, *Short-Hand Shortned,
or, The Art of Short-Writing***

London: R. Stileman, 1673; Wing (2nd edn) S5554A
152 × 98 mm

This is the only recorded copy of the sole edition of
the single book by an otherwise unknown author, the
writing master Robert Stileman. Columns and spaces
allowed the writer to add his shorthand symbols in
manuscript after printing. As Stileman neglected to do
this, his book contains no shorthand symbols. From
the rules formulated in the first third of the extant text,
it is clear that he followed old geometric systems by
using vowels intermittently within words, with
punctuation signs for vowels at the ends of words, and
symbols for them at the beginning of words.

Like the other inventors of old geometric English
systems of shorthand, Stileman published his work in
London. Quite probably he knew other systems and
oriented himself by them, especially those of Thomas
Shelton, Theophilus Metcalfe, Simon West, Job
Everardt and Elisha Coles. All these systems except
Coles's were first published between 1626 and 1658
and were available in London in Stileman's time, some
in later editions. Coles could well have been writing at
the same time as Stileman, although his *The Newest,
Plainest and the Shortest Short-Hand* first appeared in
1674, a year after Stileman, and includes Stileman in its
list of stenographic authors.

Stileman's system assigns words to phonetic
symbols. The choice of words is noticeably similar to
Metcalfe's (for example, 'c' for 'can', 'k' for 'king', 's' for
'sin') and also to West's and Shelton's. The systems
based on Jeremiah Rich assign completely different
words to the symbols. John Willis (the 'father of shorthand'), Coles and Everardt assign none at all but do
use ideograms – absent from Shelton's *Zeiglographia*
and Metcalfe – abundantly, such as a heart for the
word 'heart'. West uses some arbitrary symbols for
words, but not on the basis of ideograms. Stileman
applies ideograms sparingly (heart, compass, cross,
world).

Metcalfe, Shelton and West list abbreviations for
prefixes and suffixes, for books of the Bible and for
recurrent phrases in sermons. Stileman has symbols
for none of these. The style of writing differs markedly
from that used by Rich and his followers. Stileman's
system, while closely resembling Metcalfe's and
Shelton's stenographic best-sellers, must have been
an invention. Lack of detail renders it insignificant
and obscure, unmentioned in histories of shorthand,
although his textbook is a bibliophilic delight.

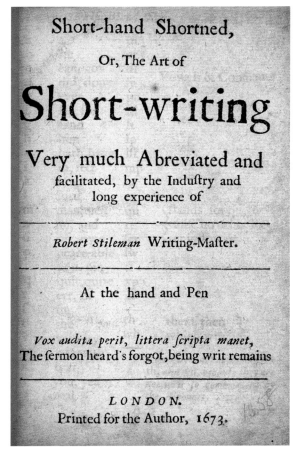

22.1

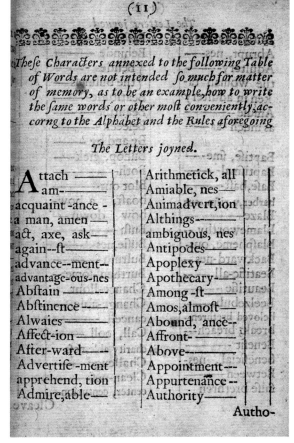

22.2

22.3

22.4

22.5

22.1 title-page

22.2 p. 11, showing columns with spaces for the manuscript addition of shorthand symbols

22.3 Henry Dix, *A New Art of Brachygraphy* (London, 1633), table showing manuscript shorthand

22.4 Thomas Shelton, *Zeiglographia* (1650), p. 32, showing woodcut shorthand symbols

22.5 William Mason, *Arts Advancement* (London, 1682), p. 8, showing engraved shorthand

23

The Case of Elizabeth Perkins, Wife of Edmund Perkins, Esquire

with

The Case of Edmund Perkins, Esq; Concerning a Bill Preferred in Parliament by Elizabeth his Wife

and

The Reply of Elizabeth Perkins, to the Case of Edmund Perkins, Esq; Concerning a Bill Preferr'd in Parliament for the Education of her Five Children in the Protestant Religion [London: s.n., 1701]

334 × 202 mm

The Case of Elizabeth Perkins is a half-folio broadside published in April 1701 explaining and advertising Perkins's legal petition (a formal printed document addressed to one vested with authority). Elizabeth Perkins, *née* Henslow, was a minor heiress who had been married in 1691, at the age of fifteen, to Edmund Perkins, a Roman Catholic. Although the estate that Elizabeth brought to the marriage was by pre-nuptial agreement entailed on her issue (that is, it was agreed that her children would inherit the estate), Edmund Perkins sold the estate in 1697 for £6,700, settling on her a jointure of £200 per annum for life. In her *Case*, Elizabeth further maintained that Edmund mistreated her during their marriage and, at some time in 1700, had taken her five children away to a distant house in Devon, where, Elizabeth argued, he was educating them in the Roman Catholic religion and planned to spirit them away to a Catholic seminary in France. Her broadside advertised that she had preferred a private bill in Parliament, asking that the law lords, specifically the Lord Chancellor and Lord Keeper (Sir Nathan Wright), might have guardianship of her children, with the charge for their education and maintenance to be levied on Edmund. Elizabeth's case rested on the penal laws against Catholics in England in this period: the children of a mixed marriage between a Protestant and a Catholic were required to be raised as Protestants and were forbidden to be sent abroad to evade this restriction ('An Act for the further preventing the Growth of Popery' 11 William III. Cap. 4).

Such is Elizabeth's argument. There is evidence that the marital dispute between husband and wife in this case, however, has more complicated origins than her petition allows. Their marriage seems to have reached an irreconcilable breakdown in the summer of 1700, for on 13 June Edmund took the serious step of advertising in the newspapers (*Post Boy*, repeated weekly from that date) that his wife had absented herself, had brought a Chancery suit against him, and that he would no longer be liable for her debts. He published a broadside reply to her petition, *The Case of Edmund Perkins Esq; Concerning a Bill Preferred in Parliament by Elizabeth his Wife*, arguing that, although the marriage had been happy for the first seven years, in 1698 she began an affair or 'Scandalous

THE
CASE
OF
Elizabeth Perkins, Wife of *Edmund Perkins*, Esquire.

THAT *Thomas Henslow*, Esquire, lately deceased, was, in his Lifetime seiz'd in Fee Simple of an Estate of the yearly Value of Six Hundred Pounds and upwards, well stored with Wood and Timber : (the said *Thomas Henslow* descending from Ancestors who were of the Protestant Religion) And being so seiz'd, had Issue only two Daughters, *Katharine* and *Elizabeth*, and afterwards died ; the said *Katherine* and *Elizabeth* surviving their said Father, and being at the time of his Decease Infants of tender Years.

That after the Decease of the said *Thomas Henslow*, *Edmund Perkins*, late of *Winckton* in *Hamshire*, intermarried with the said *Elizabeth*, one of the Daughters and Coheirs of the said *Thomas Henslow* ; the said *Elizabeth* being at the time of her Marriage an Infant about Fifteen Years of Age ; and the said *Edmund Perkins* being then and yet a Roman Catholick.

That the said *Edmund Perkins*, in right of the said *Elizabeth*, possessed himself of her Moyety of the said Estate, descended, as aforesaid, to the said *Elizabeth*, from her said Father ; and hath since sold and disposed of the same to *Richard Norton*, Esquire, or some other Person or Persons, for the Summ of Six Thousand Seven Hundred Pounds, contrary to the Agreement expressed and declared upon Marriage ; by which the said Moyety of the said Estate, descended, as aforesaid, to the said *Elizabeth*, was to remain unsold, and to descend to the Issue of the said *Edmund*, by the said *Elizabeth*.

That the said *Edmund Perkins* being, as aforesaid, a Roman Catholick, hath upon account of Religion, imposed great Hardships upon the said *Elizabeth* ; and for several Years past, used her in a very cruel and unnatural manner, the said *Elizabeth* being a Protestant of the Church of *England*, as by Law Establish'd ; and descended, as aforesaid, of a Protestant Family.

That the said *Edmund Perkins* hath had Issue by the said *Elizabeth* five Children, viz. *Elizabeth*, *Lucey*, *Francis*, *Mary*, and *Edmund*, who are now all Infants of tender Years ; and the said *Edmund Perkins* (with intent to breed and educate the said *Elizabeth*, *Lucey*, *Francis*, *Mary*, and *Edmund*, the Infants, in the Roman Catholick Religion) hath taken away and removed from the said *Elizabeth*, her said Children, and caused them to be carried and conveyed to *Athelhampston* in *Dorsetshire*, being alone House not far from the Sea-shore, with design (as is reasonably to be feared) to transport them to be educated in the Popish Religion, in some Foreign School or Seminary ; and the said Infants are there committed to the Tuition and Guardianship of a Popish Priest, and others, being Papists, to the great Discomfort of the said *Elizabeth*, and to the Incouragement of the Growth of Popery in this Kingdom ; the Example whereof may be of dangerous Consequence to the Publick, if not prevented, in all just and reasonable Instances.

That the said *Elizabeth*, notwithstanding her said Fortune, is (upon account of her religion) reduced to want Necessaries ; nevertheless she is contented to submit to that Misfortune ; but humbly prays that her Children may be educated Protestants, and that some reasonable allowance may be made by the said *Edmund*, out of the Estate in his Possession, in right of the said *Elizabeth*, for their Maintenance and Education ; and to that end the said *Elizabeth* hath preferred a Bill in Parliament, to the end the Lord Chancellor or Lord Keeper for the time being, may have a Guardianship of the said Infants, allowing (out of the Estate now in the Possession of the said *Edmund Perkins*, in the right of the said *Elizabeth*) such Summs for their Maintenance and Education as shall be thought sufficient and reasonable.

conversation' with a certain Richard Bishop, alias Savage, a person of 'very ill Circumstances', who was in 1700 committed to Newgate for 'high crimes'. It was her 'private Correspondence' with Bishop that caused Edmund to remove his children to board with a Mrs Long in Athelhempston in Dorset. Moreover, he argued, she had never raised the question of religion with him, even when bringing her case in Chancery. In a further publication, *The Reply of Elizabeth Perkins, to the Case of Edmund Perkins, Esq;*, probably published in May 1701, Elizabeth reasserted her case, especially that she was an 'Affectionate and Dutiful Wife' motivated only by the desire to have her children raised in the Protestant religion. She denied any unlawful connection with Bishop, who, she said, was a schoolfellow of Perkins from the Jesuit college for English Catholic clergy at Douai, and for that reason only had been a guest in her house.

The bill was eventually brought before the House of Lords for its first reading on 21 April 1701; legal counsel were heard before the bar on 1 and 26 May, with a large number of witnesses attesting to each version of the story. Debate focused on the question of Elizabeth's religion and the nature of her relation with Bishop, the latter reinforced by incriminating private letters between the two. After debate, the lords voted against committing the bill by 29 to 19, and, after it had been read a second time, it was rejected. The law lords' decision not to intervene suggests they were not convinced that this was a case in which they might intervene in the state of matrimony, weighing the force of matrimonial laws against those of the penal laws against Catholic education. This case created a minor scandal in the period, providing an important test of the willingness of the authorities to defend, as they saw it, the Protestant religion. However, the dispute evaporated later in the year, when Edmund Perkins died (*London Post*, 19 December 1701).

These broadsides, all ephemeral and, therefore, rare, are three of some 700 English, Scottish and Irish proclamations issued between 1575 and about 1830 held in the Goldsmiths' Library of Economic Literature.

23.2

23.3

23.1 detail of broadside,
The Case of Elizabeth Perkins

23.2 detail of broadside,
The Case of Edmund Perkins

23.3 detail of broadside,
The Reply of Elizabeth Perkins

An Advertisement.

THE Author being deceased, and the Book to be Re-printed, a Friend of is, at the request of several School-masters, ath made the following Alterations and Additions:

First, Before Examples be given to all the ules, as they stand in order in *Lilly's* Gram-iar, there are, in a preliminary way, a compe-nt number of Examples fitted to the more sy and fundamental Rules, for the initiating d grounding of Young Beginners. These ules are concerning,

1. The Nominative Case and Verb.
2. The Substantive and Adjective.
3. The Accusative Case following the Verb.
4. Conjunctions Copulative and Disjunctive, at couple like Moods and Tenses.
5. The Nominative Case following the erb *Sum*.
6. The latter of two Verbs being the Infi-tive Mood.
7. The Genitive Case latter of two Sub-ntives.

24.1

24.1 fol. A2r, showing crooked printing

24.2 detail from *The Works of Geoffrey Chaucer* (Hammersmith: Kelmscott Press, 1896), p. 58, showing schoolboys from *The Prioress's Tale*

24.2

24 **John Garretson,** *English Exercises for School-Boys to Translate into Latin*

London: J. Nicholson, J. Sprint, A. Bell, S. Burrows and H. Walwyn, 1704
151 × 88 mm

Among the first printed books were editions of the Latin grammar that goes under the name of Donatus. These survive only in fragments. Schoolbooks in many editions of almost any size commonly survive in very few (and often unique) copies, sometimes imperfect. Some textbooks were printed the length and breadth of Europe and beyond, and age-old titles were exported to North America from England, including Garretson's own *The School of Good Manners*.

Schoolmasters may die, but their books live on. In England we have figures such as William Lily, author of the Latin grammar used by Shakespeare and named in Garretson's introduction; William Camden, head-master, historian and herald; Thomas Farnaby, friend of Jonson and Selden; and many others, some running great schools, others their own establishments. Of John Garretson, who ran his own school, we know nothing, but this little book, a sequence of graded exercises for translation, is a perfect example of a tenacious title. Of this particular edition, described as the tenth, no other copy is known. A 'third edition' of 1691, printed for Thomas Cockerill (Wing G272A), is recorded in one copy, and this bears a licence dated 7 September 1686. One must presume that between 1686 and 1691 two editions are lost, and another three between 1691 and 1698, the date of the surviving 'seventh edition'. The book was still being printed in London in a twenty-fourth edition in 1777, and in Dublin in a 'twenty-first' edition in 1788. Such books were used to death, which accounts for the frequency of editions and the extreme rarity of individual copies, and, sometimes pirated, made, if not fortunes, at least respectable sums for publishers.

Garretson's contents include the type of moralising statements found in Latin textbooks over the ages and also in his *School of Good Manners*, such as 'Love thou God' (p. 4) and 'He that learneth diligently shall soon excel his companions, that play always' (p. 46), as well as historical snippets and an invective against low-calibre scholars:

Scholars go from school to Oxford or to Cambridge, that beside the learned languages, they may study the liberal arts. But some are of so stupid brains, that after that they have continued there, in the Universities, many years, they become nothing more learned, which is greatly to be wondred at; but those that are unteachable at school, for the most part continue such. (p. 89)

25 François de Salignac de La Mothe-Fénelon, *Le Avventure di Telemaco Figiuolo d'Ulisse, Ovvero Continuazione del Quarto Libro della Odissea d'Omero*

Venice: L. Pavino, 1717
171 mm × 112 mm

In 1689 Fénelon was appointed tutor to the bright but 'terrible' young Duc de Bourgogne, grandson of Louis XIV. It is for him that Fénelon composed *Les Aventures de Télémaque, Fils d'Ulysse* around 1694. The tale narrates the moral and political education of a young prince destined to rule. Influenced by the great Classical writers, *Télémaque* fills the gap between *Odyssey* IV and XV by imagining the adventures of Telemachus and his tutor Mentor (actually the goddess Minerva in disguise). *Télémaque* was both pedagogical novel and political treatise. It theorised a 'republican' monarchy based on simplicity, moderation, pacifism and wisdom.

Although enjoyed by his grandson, *Télémaque* did not amuse the Sun King, who read it as a satire on his bellicosity and luxuriousness. The first printed edition, produced in Paris in 1699, was halted by '*ordre supérieur*' before the completion of the fifth book. Having already attracted Louis's displeasure through his controversial espousal of a 'disinterested love of God', Fénelon was stripped of his tutorship and never set foot in Paris again. Louis's grandson died in 1712, and with him Fénelon's dream of an enlightened ruler.

Télémaque was spectacularly successful, being the most widely read work of its time. The approbation to the 1717 edition, edited by Fénelon's great nephew, expressed the wish that it be widely translated, and this it certainly was, into no fewer than forty languages, including Swedish (1721), Latin (1743), Russian (1747) and Polish (1750). At least 200 editions were printed by the time of the French Revolution.

The first Italian translation of *Télémaque* appeared in Leiden in 1704. This 1717 edition, the third published in Venice by Luigi Pavino, is a rarity, the only recorded copy in any English-speaking country. Based on the 1701 French edition of Adriaen Moetjens, it is dedicated to the Venetian naval hero Andrea Cornaro, who had thwarted a Turkish attack on Corfu in July 1716.

This volume was sold at the Rufford Abbey sale in 1938 and purchased by Frederick Stroud Read, first Warden of the University of London Union and an avid book collector, in January 1939. It came to the Library in July 1942 with 2,680 other volumes from Read's collection as a gift from his widow, Charlotte.

25.1 title-page and frontispiece

25.1

26.1

26 Franz Michael Regenfuss, *Auserlesene Schnecken, Muschelen und andre Schaalthiere*

Copenhagen: [s.n.], 1758
Copy produced for Frederick V of Denmark and Norway
625 × 456 mm

Auserlesene Schnecken, Muschelen und andre Schaalthiere ('Exquisite Conchs and other Snails'), by illustrator Franz Michael Regenfuss (*c.* 1712–1780), is a rare and royal publication, having been printed for King Frederick V of Denmark and Norway. The red frontispiece portrait of the King shows this copy from the London Institution to be one of the copies especially produced for Frederick to present to others; the frontispiece in the ordinary copies was blue.

The depictions of shells were exquisitely hand-coloured by the illustrator's wife, Margaretha Helena Regenfuss. Not only do they accurately portray the shells' significant taxonomic features, but they also highlight their status as rare and beautiful objects. Depicting the front and back of each shell also indicates their chirality or 'handedness', whereby one part is not superposable on its mirror image.

For learned persons in high society, the collection of exotic natural history specimens was as much about entertainment and status as scientific study. Denmark had a long history of such wonder cabinets, or *Kunstkammer*. One of the most famous examples was the cabinet of 'Wormius' or Ole Worm (1588–1654),

a professor at the University of Copenhagen. Worm published a lavishly illustrated book about his collection, the *Museum Wormiamum* (Amsterdam, 1655), and though a more luxurious production, Regenfuss's work is in the same tradition.

Regenfuss was born in Nuremberg, Germany, and enjoyed some renown as a painter and engraver. Count Adam Gottlob von Moltke (1710–1792), who also had a significant cabinet of shells, brought Regenfuss's talents to the attention of King Frederick. Regenfuss came to Copenhagen in 1754 and subsequently became the Royal Engraver. Although he obtained the privilege of editing the *Auserlesene Schnecken*, the text was written by several authors, including C. G. Kratzenstein (1723–1795), L. Spengler (1720–1807) and O. F. Müller (1730–1784), who wrote the descriptions of shells. P. Ascanius (1723–1803) compiled the lists of the shells' nomenclature, and the court chaplain, J. A. Cramer, wrote a chapter concerning the Creator's role in nature. Cramer stated: 'even if one has seen only a few beautiful shells, one should give the artist the credit he deserves for having reproduced Nature to such a point that it is doubtful whether art could come any closer.' He did not exaggerate. Regenfuss's illustrations combine fine drawing, engraving, careful rendering of drop shadows and subtle colouring to produce distinctive, accurate and three-dimensional impressions of these exquisite objects from the natural world.

26.1 tailpiece, p. LXXVII

26.2 frontispiece

26.3 (overleaf) plate 5

26.4 (overleaf) plate 8

26.2

FIG. 49.

FIG. 50.

FIG. 50.

TAB. V.

FIG. 52.

FIG. 51.

FIG. 52.

FIG. 53.

FIG. 54.

FIG. 54.

FIG. 56.

FIG. 56.

FIG. 55.

FIG. 57.

FIG. 57.

FIG. 49.

FIG. 58.

FIG. 58.

TAB. VIII.

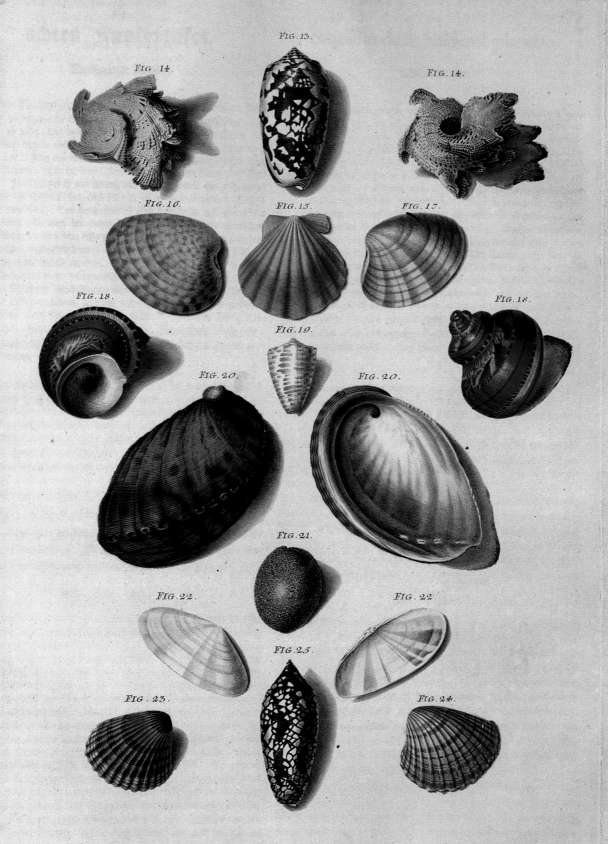

FIG. 13.

FIG. 14.

FIG. 14.

FIG. 16.

FIG. 15.

FIG. 17.

FIG. 18.

FIG. 19.

FIG. 18.

FIG. 20.

FIG. 20.

FIG. 21.

FIG. 22.

FIG. 22.

FIG. 25.

FIG. 23.

FIG. 24.

26.4

27 *Love and Honour, or, The Adventures of Serinda,*
a Beautiful Slave
Liverpool: printed and sold by S. Nevett,
[between 1802 and 1808]
176 × 108 mm

Love and Honour is a short oriental tale printed by
the Liverpool printer and bookseller Samuel Nevett.
This sixpenny, exceptionally poorly printed, copy is the
only one recorded in Britain, although copies exist of
a different version of the pamphlet published by J. Lee
in London in 1802, *The Adventures of Gen. Hutchinson
and Serinda, the Fair Georgian.*

    Love and Honour is an example of late eighteenth-
and early nineteenth-century manifestations of the
oriental tale, in which, as Ros Ballaster has argued in
Fabulous Orients (Oxford, 2005), 'the eastern tale
metamorphoses into a conduct fiction […] a parable
about the formation of modern Enlightenment
subjectivity' (pp. 142–3). The main story relates the
history of Serinda, the educated daughter of a
Georgian merchant, who is kidnapped and sold into a
harem in Aleppo, from which she is eventually rescued
by a fellow prisoner, Osmond, an officer in the Russian
army (Hutchinson in the 1802 pamphlet). The pair
escape to Russia and marry, only for Osmond to go
missing, presumed dead, on his next campaign. The
frame narrative directs the story's moral firmly at its
English female readership: Serinda's audience consists
of two new friends, Miss Waller and Miss Martin, and
her daughter by Osmond, Caroline, who listen to the
tale in the garden of Serinda's new home in Richmond.
Through both the authorial voice and Serinda's
instructional asides, the text emphasises the benefits
of being a woman in England, 'where woman is treated
like a rational being', in comparison with 'the violation
of female liberty, so general throughout the Turkish
dominions' (p. 13). The 1802 volume extends the frame
narrative by thirteen pages, in which Hutchinson
returns, and the family move to Ireland.

    The frame narrative is set in the spring or summer
of 1800, just under a year before Paul I annexed eastern
Georgia. The main action is set in the context of the
Russo-Turkish wars of the late eighteenth century,
although internal discrepancies make dating
uncertain. The text's political affiliations are, however,
clear: Serinda's Georgian father is a Christian, and she
is educated by a much-loved English governess; the
Turks enslave her, and the 'Russians' free her (Osmond
and Hutchinson are, in fact, Irish). Catherine II is
represented as intelligent and generous, in asking
Serinda's advice on 'Asiatic manners, particularly our
mode of educating females, and the treatment of
women in the harems' (p. 30), and providing her with
a pension.

27.1

27.1 frontispiece

27.2 detail of p. 23,
with blotchy printing

(23)

began to descend——My fears were renewed ; and
when I was about half way down, I imagined that
the hooks were giving way——I made an effort to shriek
but fortunately my voice was suppressed by terror
——I clung to the ladder, and remained a few seconds
suspended between heaven and earth, in a state of
stupefaction. Love reanimated my spirits, I regained my presence of mind, and with cautious steps,
reached the street.

    "The liveliest joy now inspired my soul——I step-
ped lightly along the foot-way on tiptoe, to the adjacent mosque, where, by the feeble glimmer of a
lamp, I beheld my dear deliverer waiting behind a

27.2

James Corton Cowell, 'Some Reflections on the Life of William Shakespeare: A Paper Read before the Ipswich Philosophic Society, 7 February [–April] 1805'
256 × 208 mm; MS294

The so-called 'Cowell manuscript' purportedly contains two lectures on Shakespeare's biography delivered by James Cowell to the Ipswich Philosophical Society in 1805. In the first, Cowell describes his efforts to learn more about Shakespeare's life, even travelling to Stratford-upon-Avon to see what he can discover. It turns out, very little. Cowell's growing scepticism is confirmed by an unnamed 'ingenious gentleman' with whom he spoke there, who proposed that the plays were actually written by Sir Francis Bacon (and the original manuscripts 'destroyed to conceal the fact'). The second lecture, dated April 1805, picks up where the previous one left off, although now, Cowell explains, he has been given permission to name his source, the clergyman and scholar James Wilmot (1726–1807). Wilmot, we learn, had 'devoted years to searching for some light on this great mystery' of the authorship of the plays, 'but had found only that the young man Shakespeare was at best a Country clown'. Cowell is persuaded by this and other arguments, and adds some of his own against Shakespeare and in favour of Bacon's authorship.

The revelations contained in the Cowell manuscript came to widespread attention in 1932, when the Shakespeare scholar Allardyce Nicoll published an article in the *Times Literary Supplement* entitled 'The First Baconian'. Until this time, claims that Sir Francis Bacon was the true author of Shakespeare's plays dated no earlier than the 1840s. In quoting Cowell on James Wilmot's investigations into the authorship question, Nicoll was now able to date the case for Bacon back to 1785.

While doubts about the manuscript were immediately expressed and continued to be (Cowell's geography was suspect; no one was able to identify Cowell or anyone else named in the lectures besides Wilmot; apparently no Ipswich Philosophical Society existed before 1842; etc.), Nicholl's conclusions were broadly accepted and shaped subsequent accounts of the history of the authorship controversy.

It was not until 2010 that the Cowell manuscript was exposed as a forgery. Its author or authors had slipped up when arguing that 'it is strange that Shakespeare whose best years had been spent in a profitable and Literary vocation should return to an obscure village [...] and take up the very unromantic business of a Money lender and dealer in Malt.' No one knew in 1805 that Shakespeare had dealt in malt or lent money; that information was only subsequently discovered and widely circulated.

The identity of the forger(s) is yet to be discovered.

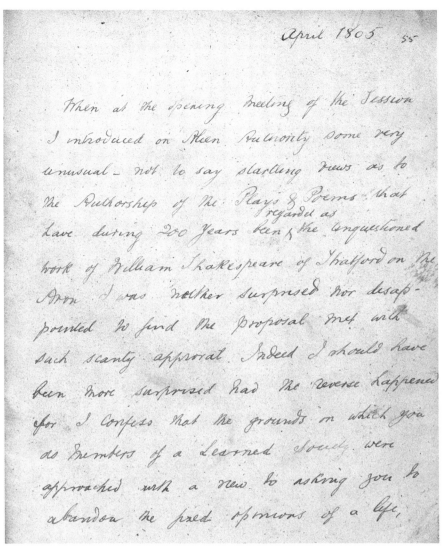

28.1

28.1 fol. 55r, with the beginning of the second lecture

28.2 Sir Francis Bacon, *Essayes and Counsels* (1664), detail of frontispiece, showing Bacon

28.2

29 Emilie Berrin, *Secretair der Liebe, oder, Galante Hieroglyphen*

Leipzig: Industrie-Comptoir, 1808

230 × 169 mm

Born in France, Emilie Berrin moved to Leipzig in 1798. There she co-edited a fashion magazine. Berrin produced several *Modellbücher*, or 'pattern books', such as the *Secretair der Liebe*, and states in her preface to this book that her hieroglyphs have had to be reprinted several times. Yet her works are unknown in Britain except for this item, held only at Senate House Library, and the magazine *Charis* at the National Art Library. They can be traced only in a very few French and German libraries because, as Berrin intended, their designs were cut up to decorate household or personal objects, or to use as valentines. The earliest extant edition of the *Secretair der Liebe* dates from 1800.

The full title translates as 'Writer of love, or, Gallant rebuses, with garlands, festoons, flowers and other decorations serving for embroidery and painting on porcelain, to express one's feelings, wishes and loves, explained by figures, to one's friends'. The three parts have twelve plates each, all exquisitely hand-coloured and embellished with floral and butterfly motifs, engraved by Charles Martin. The introductory text is followed by a simple translation of the hieroglyphs into German and French and a detailed explanation of how that translation can be deduced from the combinations of images, musical notes, letters and figures that make up the hieroglyphs.

Berrin devises elaborate vignettes, such as one for using hieroglyphs 159 and 160 on plate 20, a potentially scandalous letter between young lovers which can equally be read as an epistle from a Reverend Father to the young girl's aunt. Her hieroglyphs are simultaneously pedagogical in intent: Berrin hopes that they will succeed in teaching German children the French language where other grammars fail, and be to foreign-language teaching what spices and essences are for use in cooking or in the celebration of the Mass, removing the insipid and the bitter from the experience and instead quickening the appetite to learn. Particularly lovely are the labyrinths represented by plates 4, 6 and 8 of the second part, resembling the English endless or true-love knot which was the stock-in-trade from the mid-eighteenth century of German emigrants to Pennsylvania, where these designs are thought to have originated.

29.1 plate 8, with a labyrinth resembling an English true-love knot

29.2 details of plate 20, with vignettes for using hieroglyphs

29.3 plate 16, with vignettes for using hieroglyphs

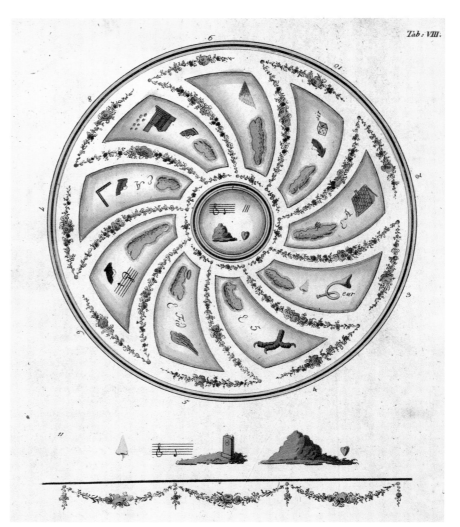

29.1

29.2

Tab. XVI.

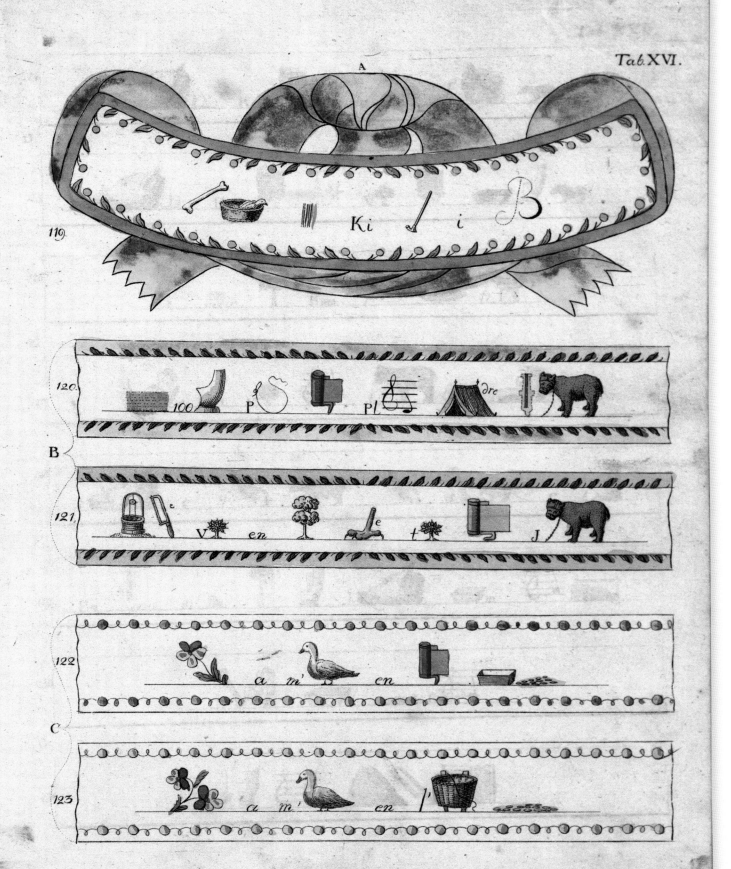

30 Charles Lamb (ed.), *Specimens of English Dramatic Poets, who Lived about the Time of Shakespeare*

London: Longman, Hurst, Rees and Orme, 1808
Presentation copy to Robert Southey
196 × 133 mm

Charles Lamb described his *Specimens of English Dramatic Poets, who Lived about the Time of Shakespeare* as being 'such a book that I am glad there should be'. The purpose of the volume was, according to Lamb's friend Thomas Noon Talfourd, to 'renew [in the English public] a taste for the great contemporaries of Shakespeare'. The book contains Lamb's selections of scenes from the plays of Elizabethan and Jacobean dramatists, and did, to some extent, prompt a resurgence of interest in Shakespeare's largely forgotten contemporaries. Lamb's concise notes on the plays were singled out for praise by contemporary reviewers, and later by George Saintsbury and Edgar Allan Poe.

The Senate House Library copy of the *Specimens* is a presentation copy, inscribed in Robert Southey's hand: 'R. Southey from the Editor, Keswick. Aug. 6. 1808.' Lamb had been introduced to Southey by Samuel Taylor Coleridge in 1795, and the two men became friends and correspondents. Lamb visited Southey in Keswick in 1802. Like the other members of the Lake School (Coleridge and William Wordsworth), Lamb and Southey often lent and borrowed books to and from each other and commented on each other's literary works. Lamb may have given the book to Southey in person, as a mark of their friendship, though he more probably asked their shared publisher, Longman, to send Southey the work.

The book originally formed part of what Southey called his 'Cottonian library', a collection of books bound by members of his family, using whatever materials they had to hand (such as old dresses previously worn by the Southey ladies). The name was given in joking homage to the Cottonian library collected by the seventeenth-century bibliophile Sir Robert Cotton, but was also perhaps a reference to the fabric – cotton – in which some of the books were bound. Lamb's *Specimens* is bound in flowered beige calico cloth.

The item was sold, uncut, as lot 1592 in the auction of Southey's library by Sotheby's in May 1844. The copy contains the Carlingford bookplate and the inscription 'C. P. Fortescue 1870' – i.e., the Liberal politician Chichester Samuel Parkinson-Fortescue (1823–1898), Baron Carlingford. Presumably it was sold on or given to Fortescue in the years following the auction. Sir Louis Sterling acquired the book in November 1930 for £198, with the boards still uncut. It has been identified as a treasure of Sterling's collection since the first printed description of his library appeared in the *Times Literary Supplement* in 1932.

30.1

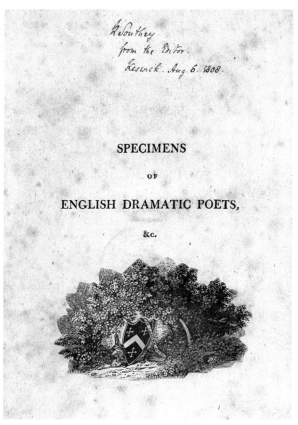

30.2

30.1 upper board, covered with flowered calico

30.2 detail of half-title, with Southey's inscription

31 **Letter from Harriet Lewin about George Grote**
25 August 1818
184 × 112 mm; MS811/1/4

Harriet Lewin (1792–1878) wrote the kind of letters that researchers delight to discover in family archives: informal, articulate and peppered with news, opinions and references to friends and family. In this letter of 25 August 1818 to her sister, written when Harriet was twenty-six years old, she shows herself fully at ease with the medium of correspondence. Her account of her 'exceeding uncomfortable Situation' is told with confidence and humour, aimed to engage her reader.

She describes a life of domestic constraint, having been forbidden to visit friends in the country. This regime followed her recent engagement to George Grote, in the face of his father's opposition and her own parents' lack of support. Although she articulates a sense of isolation and talks of the effects on her health, she writes with passion and humour about her predicament, 'bottled up and clapper clawed'. Already, it seems she is enjoying the intellectual challenge of Grote's trust that she will be 'a companion in his most exalted pursuits'.

Reading this letter with the benefit of hindsight, we can anticipate her later career as an independent thinker, the formidable wife of George Grote (1794–1871), politician and writer. Harriet was already well educated and accomplished when she first met George in 1815, but his literary and philosophical interests, pursued within a network of like-minded friends, had begun to guide her intellectually in new directions by the time they married in 1820. As his political role matured, contemporaries recognised her contribution to his success. Her posthumous biography, *The Personal Life of George Grote* (1873), demonstrates her intimate involvement in his public career and her role within his circle.

A letter will often depend on the richness of its archival context to give it meaning. In this case, although the Lewin Papers clarify the family background, the archive focuses on the career of her nephew, the Indian administrator Thomas Herbert Lewin (1839–1916). Harriet's historical significance has fortunately ensured that we know the key elements of her biography. This engaging letter illustrates how a single item of correspondence can enrich the historical narrative, enabling a personal voice to be heard.

31.1 pp. 2–3, with Harriet Lewin's description of her situation

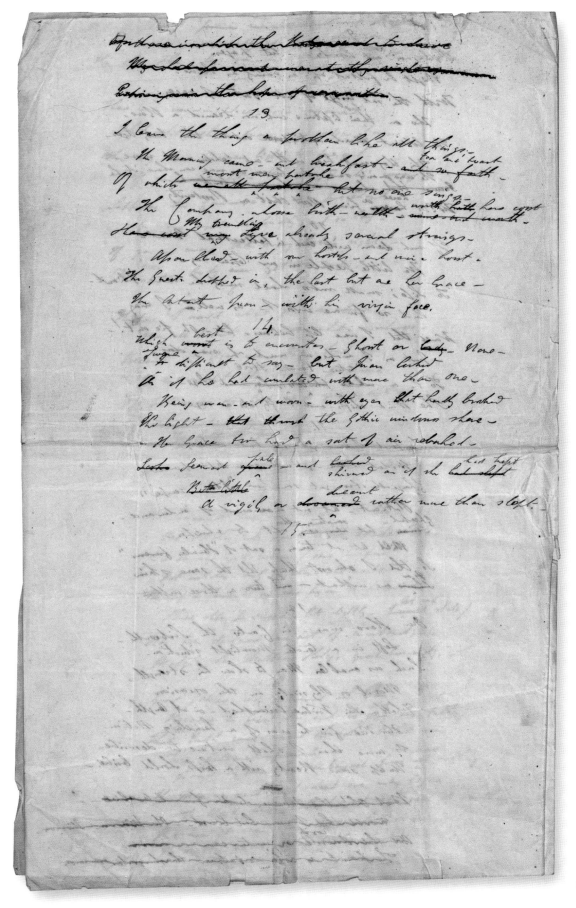

32 Holograph manuscript of Lord Byron, *Don Juan*, Canto XVII

1823

434 × 260 mm; SL.V.9

Among the liveliest of the Senate House manuscript treasures must be the autograph drafts of Byron's epic *Don Juan*, purchased by Sir Louis Sterling for a total of £9,200 in September 1936. In addition to a great many printed works by Byron, the Sterling collection contains six cantos of *Don Juan* entirely in Byron's hand and one of the three fair copies of the third canto of *Childe Harold*, the copy made by Mary Shelley with corrections by Byron.

Canto XVII is the final incomplete instalment of *Don Juan*. It is dated 8 May 1823, when Byron was planning his expedition to Greece. Lady Blessington, who kept a record of her conversations with Byron in Genoa, wrote on 10 May: 'Byron talks of going to Greece and made many jests of his intention of turning soldier. The excitement of this new mode of life seems to have peculiar attractions for him.' Yet, however distracted he was by his preparations, the manuscript shows Byron's usual meticulous respect for the traditional layout of his *ottava rima* stanza and the careful insertion of a factual footnote about the Italian word for 'bastard'. (Byron maintained an exaggerated respect for 'fact' to separate his work from the airy fictions of his contemporaries.)

The canto begins characteristically with a digression on orphans, freedom of speech and the narrator's personal difficulty in living up to the Stoic ideal. Byron then returns to Juan the morning after the night before, deletes a stanza on the perils of 'Oh Woman – Woman' and opts to 'leave the thing a problem like all things'. Byron's turn to the quotidian is primarily what separates *Don Juan* from the transcendental aspirations of other Romantic poems: 'The Morning came – and breakfast – <and so forth> tea and toast – / Of which <we all partake> most men partake but no one sings' (XVII, 13). After singing of the ravaged condition of his hero in stanza 14, Byron writes the stanza number '15.', but no more than that. Intriguingly, in the blank space on the last page of the manuscript one of the words that shows through the thin paper with particular clarity is the word 'Hero', coming through in reverse from stanza 12 ('Our Hero was – in Canto the Sixteenth …').

We will never know why Byron left *Don Juan* at stanza 15, but one of the things that may have caught his eye was the ghostly reverse image of 'Hero' – the figure he was looking for at the start of his poem: 'I want a Hero …'. Possibly this mottled, creased fragment of an unfinished canto holds the record of the moment when Byron decided to stop writing a story and to get on with the making of history.

32.2

33

John Bonnycastle, *The Scholar's Guide to Arithmetic*, ed. by Edwin Colman Tyson

London: J. Dove, 1828

175 × 109 mm

John Bonnycastle's *The Scholar's Guide to Arithmetic*, first published in 1780, was one of the most popular and enduring arithmetic textbooks of the time, running to seven editions even before the end of the eighteenth century. Bonnycastle taught the basic operations of arithmetic and their applications to standard commercial practices. For each type of problem Bonnycastle gave a 'Rule', without explanation, followed by several 'Examples', for students to work for themselves. Bonnycastle's examples appear repeatedly in children's copy-books from this period.

Edwin Colman Tyson (1815–1863), a retired headmaster of Christ's Hospital School, produced several works based on Bonnycastle's: keys to Bonnycastle's introductions to algebra and mensuration and to his *Guide to Arithmetic*, and editions of Bonnycastle's *Guide to Arithmetic* and *Introduction to Practical Geometry and Mensuration*. In his new edition of *The Scholar's Guide to Arithmetic*, apparently the earliest of his labours connected with Bonnycastle, Tyson reordered much of the material. He also introduced new examples, although many of Bonnycastle's original questions remain. Although Tyson claimed on the title-page that he would give the proofs of each rule, in general he offered no further pedagogical explanation than Bonnycastle had done. He did include two new appendices: on weights and

This book was sent to me by the publisher, meaning to call my attention to it as a class book. It convinced me that a work on demonstrative arithmetic was wanting — and was the book which suggested the ~~exact~~ existence of the deficiency to supply which I wrote my own arithmetic in 1830

AdeMorgan

Sept. 15, 1857

THE

SCHOLAR'S GUIDE

TO

ARITHMETIC:

WITH NOTES,

CONTAINING THE PROOF OF EACH RULE.

TOGETHER WITH

SOME OF THE MOST USEFUL PROPERTIES OF NUMBERS.

By JOHN BONNYCASTLE,

PROFESSOR OF MATHEMATICS IN THE ROYAL MILITARY ACADEMY, WOOLWICH.

ENLARGED AND IMPROVED BY THE

REV. E. C. TYSON, M.A.

FELLOW OF CATHARINE HALL, CAMBRIDGE, AND LATE HEAD MASTER IN THE ROYAL MATHEMATICAL SCHOOL, CHRIST'S HOSPITAL.

"Dicat
Filius Albini, si de quincunce remota est
Uncia, quid superat? poteras dixisse—Triens: Eu!
Rem poteris servare tuam: redit uncia; quid fit?
Semis."—HOR.

LONDON:

PRINTED AND PUBLISHED BY J. F. DOVE,

ST. JOHN'S SQUARE.

1828.

measures, to take account of the new Imperial system introduced in 1824; and tables for the calculation of annuities, a subject he also treated at length in the text.

Tyson's edition does not appear to have been widely adopted. It is known to have been printed only once more, by William Tegg in 1848, while Bonnycastle's original continued into several further editions up to 1851. Today, Tyson's edition of 1828 is very rare, with only two copies known to exist in British libraries. The copy shown is particularly noteworthy because it belonged to Augustus de Morgan and carries a note by him on the flyleaf:

This book was sent to me by the publisher, meaning to call my attention to it as a class book. It convinced me that a work on demonstrative arithmetic was wanting – and was the book which suggested the existence of the deficiency to supply which I wrote my own arithmetic in 1830.
A De Morgan
Sept. 15, 1857.

The book to which De Morgan referred was his own *The Elements of Arithmetic*, published in 1830, in which he aimed to teach the rules of arithmetic 'accompanied by the reasoning'. When De Morgan wrote of pupils 'toiling from rule to rule through countless examples, and dragging at each remove a lengthened chain', he was surely thinking back to Bonnycastle and Tyson.

That De Morgan owned both Tyson's edition and Bonnycastle's 1780 publication is no oversight: De Morgan owned several runs of editions of popular textbooks, from Robert Record to William Oughtred, Edward Cocker and James Hodder.

33.2

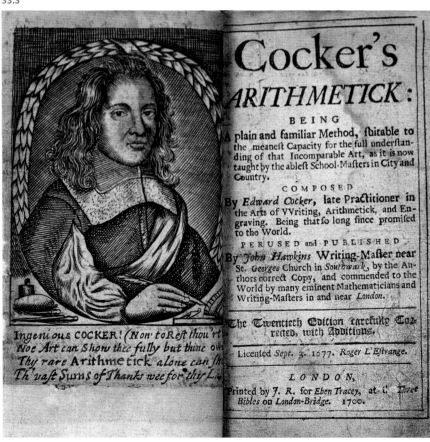

33.3

33.1 Bonnycastle, title-page and facing flyleaf, with De Morgan's note

Two popular mathematical textbooks, of which Augustus De Morgan owned several editions:

33.2 William Oughtred, *Clavis Mathematicae Denuo Limita*, 5th edn (Oxford, 1693), title-page and frontispiece

33.3 Edward Cocker, *Cocker's Arithmetick*, 20th edn (London, 1700), title-page and frontispiece

Nay be granted from Our College

34.1

34 First Charter of the University of London
1836
665 × 725 mm; UoL/ST/1/1/1

The Royal Charter of 1836 that established the University of London appears with all the colour and elegance that one would expect, because Royal Charters are special documents. Furthermore, London was only the third university in Britain to obtain a Royal Charter (albeit some 600 years after Cambridge and then Oxford received theirs), so one might have reason to anticipate a vision to match the appearance of the document. Anyone reading the entire document, which is close to 3,000 words, might be disappointed. There is little vision and a great deal on what might seem to be mundane governance and procedural matters. Yet the Royal Charter remains a historic document: historic in the sense that it was very much a product of its time, and historic in that it created what was to become a major and distinctive university.

The foundation of the University of London emerged from the religious and secular politics of the late 1820s and early 1830s. A body called London University had opened in Bloomsbury's Gower Street in 1828, aiming to educate students from middle-class backgrounds and without the religious entrance requirements of the ancient universities. It called itself a university but had no Royal Charter and did not award degrees. Anglican and Conservative opinion was roused in response, and in 1831 the new King's College opened, established by Royal Charter but without the title of university. The reforming Whig government of 1835 found the solution to the ensuing tensions in creating a University of London, with the institution in Gower Street having to change its name to University College London, and accept an equal status with King's in the new University of London.

The Royal Charter has to be understood in that context. The opening lines announce the wish 'to hold forth to all classes and denominations of Our faithful subjects, without any distinction whatsoever, an encouragement for pursuing a regular and liberal course of Education'. There were to be no religious or political tests.

The other distinctive course set out in the Charter of 1836 was that the new University existed not to educate students (it had no building, no teaching staff, no library) but to examine them and reward proficiency in literature, science and art by academic degrees. The education was to be obtained at colleges to be named by the government, initially University College and King's College. By the second Royal Charter (1858) the requirement that students who presented themselves for examination had to have studied at a specific institution was removed, allowing anyone to obtain knowledge howsoever they chose. The outcome was the External System (now International Programmes), by which means students worldwide could study and take examinations for University of London degrees. The University of London Act of 1898 was to bind the Colleges in London more closely into the University, with the latter monitoring curriculum and academic quality. Nonetheless, the University as an examining rather than a teaching body that had been set in 1836 continued to shape its character.

Another aspect of the Royal Charter's text may surprise readers. What is this long list of names that so dominates it? The Royal Charter names the Chancellor and Vice-Chancellor, as well as the thirty-eight members of the Senate. The government of the day chose those who were to govern the University, and, being a Whig government, it selected men of impressive reputation and broadly progressive ideas, most of them very eminent medical experts, scientists and lawyers. Nonetheless, it was the government of the day that would choose them, while all by-laws and regulations were to be approved by the Treasury. Contrary to common belief, government interference in universities is not merely a product of recent times.

34.2

34.1 charter

34.2 detail of top border, showing the Royal coat of arms

34.3 detail of left border, showing King William IV

34.4 detail of right border, showing Queen Adelaide

34.3

34.4

A Series of Twelve Books, by Mrs. Sherwood.

[QNL] KIO (p.c.2)
Ref only

COMFORT IN DEATH.

BY
MRS. SHERWOOD,
Author of
Duty is Safety; Frank Beauchamp; Jack
the Sailor Boy; Think before you
Act; Sisterly Love; Grandmama
Parker; Uncle Manners;
and the Traveller

LONDON:
DARTON AND CO.,
HOLBORN HILL.

Stassin et Xavier.
Libraires
Rue du Coq St.Honoré, No.9.

35.1

35

Mrs (Mary Martha) Sherwood, *Comfort in Death*
London: Darton, [between 1845 and 1848];
Dartons, H1363
145 × 121 mm

Domesticated martyrology, popular with Puritan
writers in the late seventeenth century, was revived by
the Evangelicals at the start of the nineteenth. Mrs
Sherwood, *née* Mary Martha Butt, was its most prolific
and successful purveyor. In all, she wrote some 350
titles, including *Susan Gray* (1802), whose eponymous
dying heroine, secure in her Christian faith and the
hope of salvation, chides her family for their grief and
counsels them to follow her pious example; *Little
Henry and his Bearer* (1815), about a dying eight-year-
old British boy in India who converts his servant; and
the enormously successful *The Fairchild Family*
(1818–47).

The more ephemeral *Comfort in Death* conforms
in some ways to the standard holy life/joyful death
model, finishing with an account of a four-year-old
boy's pious demise. But its tone is not stringent. Most
of its sixteen pages recount the conversation of Walter
Ellis and his mother. Their talk revolves around death,
but it touches Walter only indirectly: his pet bird was
languishing but has recovered, his former nurse is ill,
and the boy whose death closes the narrative was
Walter's uncle, who expired long ago. Much of the
tract, in fact, is about how the dead are memorialised.
Walter's mother explains that abroad – especially in
'the east' – costly tombs are raised to honour the dead,
and that in many foreign countries ordinary people are
often buried in 'fields for the dead' adorned with
monuments. These practices are contrasted with the
'quiet country churchyard in England', much preferred
by Walter. Although his mother dutifully points out

35.1 *Comfort in Death*,
front wrapper

35.2 Mrs Sherwood, *The
History of Little Henry and his
Bearer* (Wellington, Salop,
1817), engraved title-page

35.3 Mrs Sherwood, *The
History of Susan Gray* (London,
1871), p. 10

35.4 *Comfort in Death*, p. 5

WELLINGTON.
Printed by and for F. Houlston and Son 1814.
(*Entered at Stationers' Hall.*)

35.2

"At noon, when the sun was high in the heavens, and the air was warm, she would sit at the door of the house, looking around her upon the green woods, the river rolling through the meadows, and the church upon the hill, where she hoped her body would be laid beside those of her dear parents."—P. 9.

35.3

that where a body is buried matters much less than the fate of the soul, the pamphlet could be read as Sherwood's intervention in current debates on memorialisation. By the late 1840s, when the pamphlet was published, municipal cemeteries were being opened in the major cities (for example, Kensal Rise in 1832 and Highgate in 1839), and, following Prince Albert's death in 1861, mourning was to become a much more public rite. His lying in state, and the magnificent Albert Memorial, smack very much of the 'foreign' practices disparaged in *Comfort in Death*.

Comfort in Death first appeared as a single tuppenny pamphlet, and was later bundled up with the eleven other Sherwood titles in the series to form *My New Story Book* (1848). This copy was apparently retailed in France (it bears a label for the booksellers Stassin et Xavier of Paris). It is one of only two known copies.

COMFORT IN DEATH.

"MAMA," said Walter Ellis, "do just listen to that bird; why it was only this very morning it seemed so ill that Papa thought it was going to die, and now

how well it is again! Should you not say it was quite well now, Mama, and may not poor Mary Jones,

35.4

Glaucium phœniceum.

36.1

36   John Sibthorp, *Flora Graeca Sibthorpiana*
London: Richard Taylor, 1806–40 [i.e., H. G. Bohn, 1845–46]; 10 vols
500 × 354 mm

John Sibthorp was Professor of Botany at Oxford, and in March 1786 he made a journey to Greece, taking with him as botanical artist the young Ferdinand Bauer, whom he had found at the Vienna Botanic Garden. His purpose was not simply to study the flora of Greece but also to try to identify once and for all the 700 plants described in the first-century *Materia Medica* of Dioscorides, the primary work on herbal medicine from the ancient world.

Having returned to England in September 1787 (but having spent over another year botanising in Greece from March 1794 until May 1795), Sibthorp died in 1796. His *Flora* was completed by Sir James Edward Smith, the founder of the Linnean Society, with hand-coloured engraved plates based on Bauer's drawings, and elaborate title-pages, each with a Grecian scene by Bauer. The work would eventually fill ten volumes, with 966 plates, but Smith died in 1828 and was succeeded as editor by John Lindley, the Assistant Secretary of the Horticultural Society. An opponent of the Linnaean system of classification that Smith had spent his career promoting, Lindley completed the work in the manner that Smith had begun, and added in the final volume an appendix giving his version of how the plants should have been classified.

There were never more than thirty subscribers to the *Flora Graeca*, and, since some subscribers died during the thirty-plus years of its production, only twenty-five sets were completed. (Lindley could never afford a copy himself: his own copy consists solely of the letter-press for the portion he edited, with no plates.) So in 1845 the bookseller Henry G. Bohn purchased the copperplates and unsold sheets and produced a reprint of forty copies, differing somewhat in the colouring of the plates (commercially prepared pigments having become available), but reliably distinguished from the original only by the watermarks.

The Senate House copy originally belonged to the London Institution. The work is mentioned individually in the University of London Library Committee's annual report for 1925 as one of seventy-six 'items of special interest and value' received from the Institution, with the note (repeated in the Library's card catalogue) 'Only 30 complete copies of this sumptuous work were prepared and issued to subscribers': evidence that the Library believed itself to have acquired the original edition. In each volume, however, the plates bear water-marks dated 1845, proving that this is one of the forty reprinted copies.

FLORA GRÆCA

Sibthorpiana.

CENTURIA PRIMA,

1806

MONS PARNASSUS.

36.1 vol. 5, plate 189, *Glaucinum phoenicum*

36.2 vol. 1, title-page

36.3 (overleaf) vol. 5, plate 473, *Sempervivum arboretum*

36.4 (overleaf) vol. 1, plate 28, *Merina persica*

Sempervivum arboreum.

Morina persica.

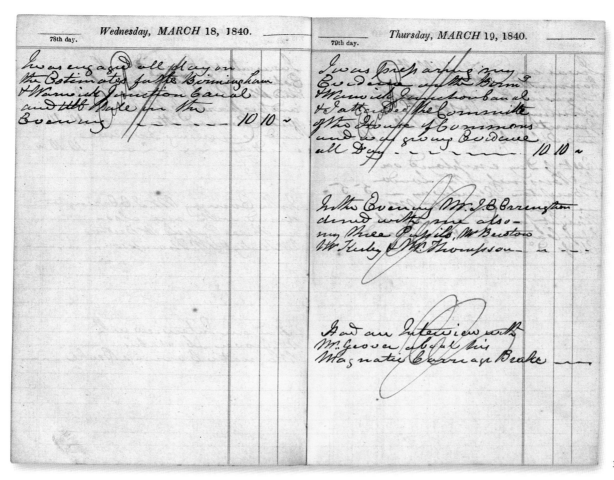

37.1

37

Diary of John Urpeth Rastrick F.R.S.
1840
201 × 123 mm; MS242

The world's first full passenger railway, running between Liverpool and Manchester, opened in 1830. The prominent civil and mechanical engineer John Urpeth Rastrick (1780–1856) had advised on it. Until 1849 he was to be involved as witness, surveyor or engineer in many railway projects in the United Kingdom. These included engineering a 'direct' route between London and Brighton. Rastrick's diary for 1840 shows the line's four-year construction period to have been the most intensive in his career.

Meticulous daily entries note everything that Rastrick undertook and everyone he met: a record that he could consult if queries arose and a means of valuing his time, which was bookable to his clients. Rastrick's clerk 'signed off' the entries as part of the invoicing process. Rastrick covered several thousand miles inspecting the works and visiting suppliers in the Midlands and north-west of England. This related to ironwork for stations, and for carriages, wagons and locomotives. Monday 28 September 1840 was a typical day for him:

I set out by the Bolton Railway from Manchester at 9 O'Clock and was with Mr. Hick about the engines and cranks &c till eleven O'Clock when I returned to Manchester and was with Mr. Roberts about the Locomotive Engines till 2 O'Clock PM. I then went to Liverpool and was engaged with Mr. Keneday [sic] Mr. Bury's Foreman till five O'Clock PM when I dined and set out by the Grand Junction Railway at 7 O'Clock PM. and got to Birmingham at half past eleven O'Clock [...] Stayed at the New Royal Hotel 5 5/-*

Despite the intensity of these duties, Rastrick continued to consider several other time-demanding canal and railway projects. He spent the morning of Thursday 22 October, for example, on various matters concerning the London and Brighton Railway (£5 5s. 0d.) until 'at three O'Clock I posted down to Woodford and Epping Place and staid [sic] all night on the London & Norwich Railway acct' (i.e., the proposed East Anglian Railway; £10 10s. 0d.).

His papers, acquired by Senate House Library in four tranches between 1908 and 1965, are an invaluable source for transport history and testimony to the energy and industry of one of its early Victorian engineering giants.

*Five-guinea fee for the day chargeable to the London & Brighton Railway

38 **Dionysius Lardner,** *Railway Economy: A Treatise on the New Art of Transport, its Management, Prospects, and Relations, Commercial, Financial, and Social*
London: Taylor, Walton and Maberly, 1850
198 × 119 mm

In a longhand inscription dated *c.* 1875, Herbert Somerton Foxwell tells us (see p. xii):

I bought this volume from a bookstall in Great Portland Street *at* Jevons' *suggestion, one afternoon as I was going to Hampstead with him, for 6d.! He urged me to buy it, partly on account of the low price, partly because it was a book of great intrinsic value, from which had suggested to him the mathematical treatment of economic theory.* […] *This purchase was the first step in the formation of my economic collection.*

Foxwell's expenditure, around £2 in today's money, following the advice of his friend William Stanley Jevons (1835–1882), a prominent British economist and logician, was the beginning of a long-lasting enterprise. With the benefit of hindsight, the treatise's systematic and comparative structure and its comprehensive analysis of one of the most transformative forces of nineteenth-century Britain, namely the railways, seemed a suitable illustration of the scope and ambition of what would become the Goldsmiths' Library of Economic Literature.

Railway Economy is a landmark in the prolific career of Dionysius Lardner (1793–1859), author of several books on science and a successful public and academic lecturer. Completed in Paris, where Lardner had lived since 1845, the treatise provides a rigorous examination of the key elements in the business of railways, making prominent use of statistics. The treatise reminds us of the relationship between transport, progress and civilisation, before exploring in detail the organisation of railways, their locomotives and rolling stock, their stations, the clearing house, their passenger and goods traffic, their expenses, receipts and accidents, and the electric telegraph. Lardner then discusses the railways, and transport more generally, in the USA, Russia and Europe. He concludes with a reflection on railways and the State, based largely on a series of parliamentary reports examining railway practices in Britain in the late 1840s.

Like most of Lardner's work, *Railway Economy* attempted to translate the intricacies of developments in science and technology into a language that was accessible to larger audiences. Excerpts from the wealth of information the treatise contained, often traffic and accident figures but also information about the other countries surveyed, were cited frequently in newspapers and other publications, which, according to *The Morning Chronicle*, made it 'exactly the book that was wanted'. More recent assessments highlight the treatise's significance for our understanding of nineteenth-century political economy. Although translations and re-issues are relatively few and recent, it is acknowledged as an economic classic.

38.1 J. W. Carmichael, *Views on the Newcastle and Carlisle Railway* (Newcastle, 1836), River Wall at Wylam Scars

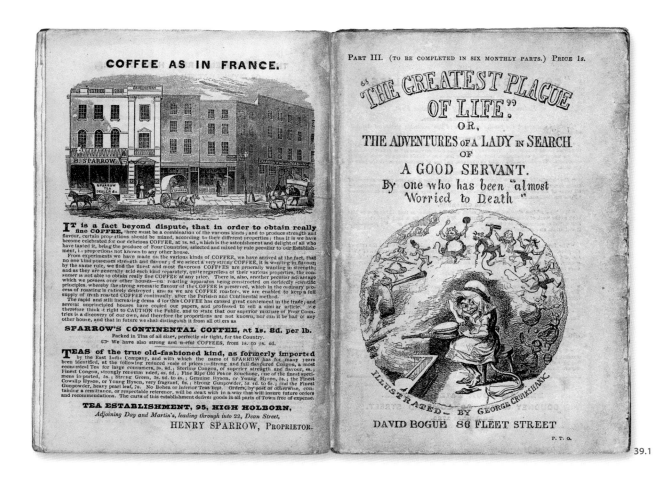

39 Henry and Augustus Mayhew, *The Greatest Plague in Life or The Adventures of a Lady in Search of a Good Servant. By one who has been 'almost worried to death*, ill. by George Cruikshank

London: D. Bogue, 1847; six monthly parts
185 × 123 mm

George Cruikshank (1792–1878) was the outstanding English political and social caricaturist of the first half of the nineteenth century and was celebrated also for his illustrations of work by Dickens (*Sketches by Boz* and *Oliver Twist*) and William Harrison Ainsworth among others. By the mid-1840s his work was less in demand. In this year Henry Mayhew (1812–1887) and his brother Augustus (1826–1875) brought to the publisher David Bogue an idea for a comic series, to be published in shilling monthly parts. It would purport to be written by the much-harassed mistress of a middle-class household and deal with the problems of recruiting and managing domestic servants, already a favourite subject of the comic weekly magazine *Punch* (founded in 1841). The Mayhews were the fourth and seventh sons of a prosperous London solicitor who had rejected their father's profession for the bohemian world of comic journalism and writing for the theatre that flourished in the London of the 1830s and 1840s.

Bogue accepted their proposal and commissioned Cruikshank to supply two etchings for each part, together with a wrapper design and title-page vignette.

The Greatest Plague in Life was a great hit, reputedly selling more copies than the monthly parts of *Pickwick Papers* had done. Cruikshank's brilliantly comic plates helped greatly in this respect. The number of advertisers taking space in such publications is always a good indication of sales, and each of the last three parts of *The Greatest Plague* features sixteen pages of advertisements for other books, pens and ink, lingerie and iron fenders among other items, in addition to cover advertisements, such as the regular ones for 'The Gentlemen's Real Head of Hair, or Invisible Ventilating Peruke' and 'The Atrapilatory, or Liquid Hair-dye'.

The success of *The Greatest Plague* encouraged Bogue to commission two further series in similar format written by the Mayhews and illustrated by Cruikshank: *Whom to Marry and How to Get Married! Or, The Adventures of a Lady in Search of a Good Husband* (1847–48) and *1851; Or, The Adventures of Mr and Mrs Sandboys* (written in 1851 by Henry Mayhew alone). The fact that Sir Louis Sterling had already acquired copies of both these works no doubt caused him to purchase this copy of *The Greatest Plague* for £22 10s. 0d. in 1930.

39.4

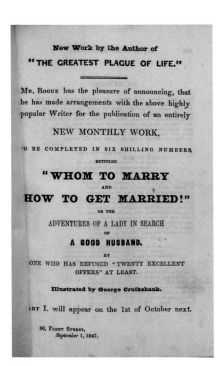

39.1 part 3, front and back cover

39.2 part 4, advertisement

39.3 advertisement inserted into Part 6 for the Mayhews' next work, *Whom to Marry and How to Get Married*

39.4 part 2, illustration by Cruikshank: ' "It's my Cousin M'am!" '

39.5 part 3, illustration by Cruikshank: 'Going out for a holiday'

Augustus De Morgan, *Formal Logic: or,*
The Calculus of Inference, Necessary and Probable
London: Taylor and Walton, 1847
Augustus De Morgan's annotated copy
228 × 143 mm

Augustus De Morgan's personal copy of his *Formal Logic* provides prime glimpses into a creative mind at work. A mathematician, mathematical historian and logician and the formulator of De Morgan's laws, De Morgan wrote and published this book in 1847, in the midst of a rush of interest in logic: it appeared just a year after his first major paper on the subject and was rendered obsolete by another paper that he published a mere three years later. The original work was a rather nondescript volume of 294 pages, swelled to 336 by the addition of an appendix, but in his office De Morgan added enough material to swell his copy to two volumes.

Striking among the scribbled notes, newspaper articles and personal letters bound into the book is a series of carefully crafted images drawn in the first months of 1853 but never published. The 45-year-old De Morgan was 'in the prime of his life for invention' when he drew these images, and was deep in the study of logic.

For De Morgan the study of logic held the key to understanding human reason: 'Every sentence in which different assertions are combined to produce another and a final assertion, is either a syllogism, a collection of syllogisms, or a mass of words without meaning. All that is called reasoning, and which cannot be made syllogistic, is not reasoning at all; and all which cannot easily be made syllogistic is obscure', he wrote in the *Penny Cyclopedia* (1842). His starting-point was Aristotelian syllogistic logic. In Aristotle's system four basic propositions could be combined to make valid syllogisms. De Morgan's first move towards

a more comprehensive system was to increase that number to eight; his next step lay in defining a logical symbology – he used parentheses and dots – that could be manipulated with all of the ease of algebra.

These aspects of De Morgan's thinking are reflected in his first diagram, dated 5 January 1853, which arranges the parentheses and dots of his eight propositional forms in a simple expansion of the traditional Aristotelian 'Table of Relations'. By 18 February, and his second page of diagrams, De Morgan had moved beyond the relations of propositions to show the relations among syllogisms. The third page, tentatively dated 21 February 1853, contains an image so large it had to be folded in three to fit into his book. The resulting triptych, when closed, displays a group of eight syllogisms that De Morgan saw as the gateway to his symbolical approach to syllogistic logic; when opened, they revealed the complex tapestry of thirty-two syllogisms that De Morgan believed encompassed all human reasoning.

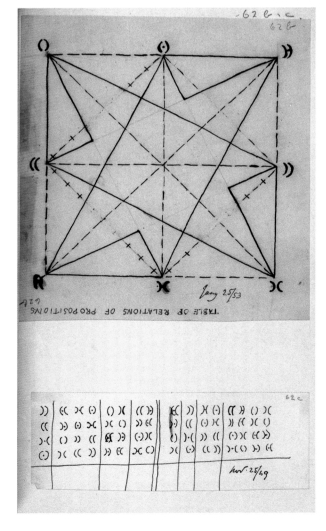

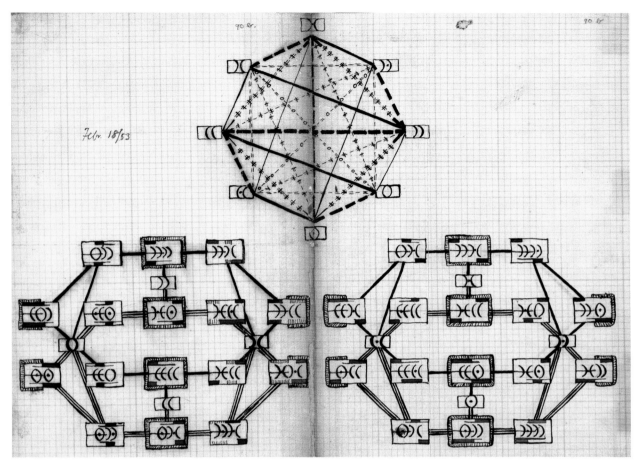

40.2

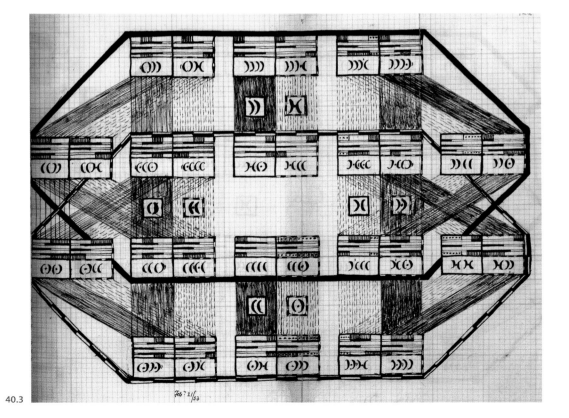

40.1 drawing by Augustus De Morgan,
'Table of relations of propositions',
25 January 1853, inserted after p. 62
of ch. 4, 'On propositions'

40.2 drawing by Augustus De Morgan,
18 February 1853, inserted after p. 90
of chapter 5, 'On the syllogism'

40.3 drawing by Augustus De Morgan,
21 February 1853, inserted after p. 92
of chapter 5, 'On the syllogism'

40.3

41.1

41   Letters from Robert and Elizabeth Barrett Browning
1855
131 × 89 mm, mounted to 279 × 216 mm; HPC/4C/3

On 23 July 1855 two famous Victorian poets, Robert and Elizabeth Barrett Browning, attended a spiritualist séance at the house of Mr and Mrs John Rymer in Ealing, west London. The presiding figure at the séance was the most renowned 'medium' of the day, the American prodigy Daniel Dunglas Home. What happened at this séance, and its aftermath, has become one of the great legends of the Brownings' marriage – including the dramatic, but untrue, story that when Home later visited the couple at their London lodgings, Robert kicked him downstairs. What is certain is that the episode put a real strain on the Brownings' relationship.

Elizabeth is writing nearly a month after the event, to a Miss de Gaudrion, who had heard of the séance and wanted to know more. Her letter is a careful, measured statement: she declares her belief that Home was not 'responsible' for the phenomena (he was simply the 'medium' through which they occurred), and she characterises such phenomena as early, imperfect signs of 'access from a spiritual world'. Her tone contrasts with the studied, stiff formality of Robert's note, couched in the third person as though he wanted to distance himself even further from a distasteful subject.

What actually happened at Ealing? We know from other letters that the 'manifestations' included rapping, movement of the table and the mysterious playing of an accordion. One detail stands out: a wreath was placed by 'spirit-hands' on Elizabeth's head, and Home was later to claim that Robert's animosity was explained by envy that this tribute had not been awarded to him. Robert does not claim here to have detected Home in the act of cheating, but argues that Home relied on psychological manipulation to disguise his physical interventions.

41.2

The explanation of the 'phenomena' lay in the willing credulity of the participants. It was inexpressibly painful to Robert that one of the victims of this credulity should be 'the best and rarest of natures' – the woman he loved.

Home did visit the Brownings a few days later, and Robert, as he says, 'relieved himself', albeit not by physical violence. And the Ealing séance had one other, far less trivial consequence. It lies behind one of the greatest of Robert's dramatic monologues, 'Mr Sludge – "the Medium"'. The poem was published in *Dramatis Personae* in 1864, three years after Elizabeth's death. It was Browning's way of having the last word in this lovers' quarrel.

41.1 Mme Dunglas Home, *D. D. Home: His Life and Mission* (London, 1888), detail of frontispiece showing Daniel Dunglas Home

41.2 letter from Robert Browning to Miss M. A. de Gaudrion, 30 August 1855, p. 1

42 The English Version of the Polyglot Bible

London: Samuel Bagster and Sons, [before 1863]

164 × 107 mm

How can we find out how people in the past were influenced by books, given that reading is essentially a private, mental activity? One way is to study how readers have annotated books. These marks reveal what it was that interested, bored, enraged or delighted them.

Among the most heavily annotated books have been Bibles, and the illustration below comes from *The English Version of the Polyglot Bible*, first published by Samuel Bagster in 1816. This copy originally belonged to Mary Hogg, wife of Sir James Hogg (1790–1876). We know from inscriptions that in 1863 she gave it to her son, the merchant and philanthropist Quintin Hogg (1845–1903), and that in 1871 he presented it to his wife, Alice, on the occasion of their marriage. It subsequently belonged to one of their daughters, Ethel Mary Wood (1876–1970), and formed part of the collection of Bibles that she deposited in Senate House Library in 1950 and bequeathed in 1970.

The annotations are in several hands, but most are by Alice Hogg. The flyleaves are covered with writing, including not only personal records such as the births, baptisms and marriages of her five children but also miscellaneous subjects for Bible lessons, moralising lists of the duties of parents, groups of biblical verses on specific topics, such as the seven 'I am' declarations of Jesus in John's Gospel, and poems, including one written for her as a girl by her father. In the body of the Bible itself, nearly every page contains marginalia revealing how it was used for private devotional reflection and study. There are quotations from popular hymns and authors such as John Bunyan, and scraps of historical information. A note on the opening words of Psalm 23 lists other references to 'our Lord as the "Shepherd" of his people'. This kind of 'concordant' reading practice, in which apparently unrelated verses are drawn together, was strongly encouraged by the layout of Bagster's Bible, where a central column on each page set out cross-references designed to demonstrate 'the harmony of the sacred writers' and the 'concurrence of the Old and New Testaments'. The annotations in this copy provide striking evidence of the variety of ways in which this Bible was read and treasured by generations of owners.

42.1 flyleaves with manuscript notes by Alice Hogg

43 **Elizabeth Barrett Browning,** *Aurora Leigh*
London: Chapman and Hall, 1857
Copy annotated by Thomas Carlyle
195 × 129 mm

Sir Louis Sterling acquired this copy of the first edition of Elizabeth Barrett Browning's narrative poem *Aurora Leigh*, annotated by Thomas Carlyle, for £30 in October 1944. An anonymous, undated accompanying typed note, with a transcript of Carlyle's fifty-nine marginal notes, explains that the book was recased at some time and that the binder wrote 'Case/Miss Aitken', a reference to Mary Aitken, Carlyle's niece (1848–1895), who kept house for him in Chelsea from 1868, two years after the death of his wife, Jane. The catalogue *The Sterling Library* (privately printed, 1954, p. 29) suggests, wrongly, that the Sterling copy of *Aurora*

Leigh was bought by Mary soon after its publication and sent to Carlyle. Mary's dates – she was a girl of eight when the poem was published – make this impossible. She must have sent the copy to the binder in later years, though before 1879, when she married her cousin Alexander Carlyle.

The copy was not Carlyle's own. On 3 February 1857 he annotated it: 'To be returned (by and by), not being properly mine'. It seems to have been sent to him by his brother John from Dumfriesshire, where he was visiting his and Carlyle's siblings, including their sister Jean Aitken. Carlyle wrote on 25 January 1857 to thank him for 'your *Aurora Leigh*'. He dismissed the poem in words familiar to the many poets and would-be poets who sent him their work in hopes of an encouraging response: 'This Lady "hath a good utterance of speech"; but as to the thing *said* with it, one asks, Is it a thing at all? – a sad pack of people these rhymesters of our time!' A few weeks later he wrote to his sister Jean, telling her to '*keep*' the poem, 'with my blessing', which suggests that the copy had travelled back to Dumfriesshire from Chelsea. It may have come into Mary Aitken's possession later, through her mother. Alternatively, the copy could be one given or lent to Carlyle by his friend and admirer John Ruskin; the sculptor Thomas Woolner, a mutual friend of the two men, told Tennyson's wife in August 1857 that Carlyle 'spoke with profound contempt of Ruskin because the little Art Deity [Ruskin] called "Aurora Leigh" the finest poem by far of the present age, and gave him a copy to read'.

Carlyle's exaggeratedly sceptical annotations to this rather overwrought work are typical of his written responses on the books he read. When the narrator or a character in the dramatic poem asks a question, Carlyle answers 'Can't say'; when the protagonist says it is 'too easy to go mad', Carlyle urges 'don't!'; beside a simile comparing torn-up paper to 'forest-leaves, stripped suddenly and rapt/by a whirlwind in Valdarno', Carlyle writes a sardonic ' "devilish fine!" ' Summing up his view at the end of Book I of the poem, he writes, 'How much better had all this been if written straight forward in clear prose utterance.' His parting shot is that the poem is 'a very beautiful tempest in a teapot'. In 1844 Elizabeth Barrett reported that Carlyle had advised her 'that a person of my "insight" and "veracity" ought to use "speech" rather than "song" in these days'. Carlyle was nothing if not consistent in his opposition to poetry as a genre.

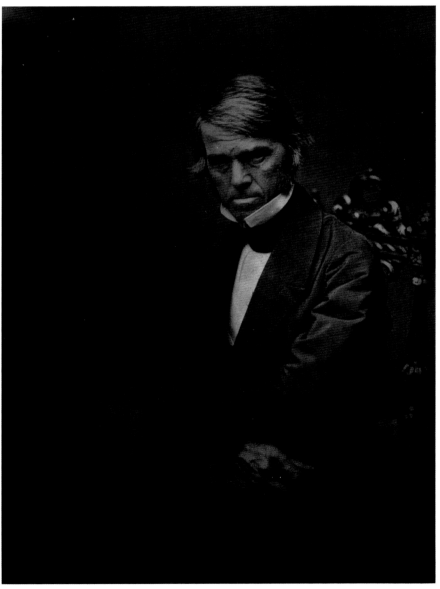

43.1 Thomas Carlyle, *Past and Present* (London, 1870), frontispiece, showing Carlyle

43.2–7 *Aurora Leigh*, details of pp. 26, 41, 164, 170, 347 and 403, annotated by Thomas Carlyle

And lived my life, and thought my thoughts, and prayed
My prayers without the vicar; read my books,
Without considering whether they were fit
To do me good. Mark, there. We get no good
By being ungenerous, even to a book,
And calculating profits . . so much help
By so much reading. It is rather when
We gloriously forget ourselves, and plunge
Soul-forward, headlong, into a book's profound,
Impassioned for its beauty and salt of truth—
'Tis then we get the right good from a book.

oh, yes

I read much. What my father taught before
From many a volume, Love re-emphasised
Upon the self-same pages: Theophrast

'And see! is God not with us on the earth?
And shall we put Him down by aught we do?
Who says there's nothing for the poor and vile
Save poverty and wickedness? behold!'
And ankle-deep in English grass I leaped,
And clapped my hands, and called all very fair.

In the beginning when God called all good,
Even then, was evil near us, it is writ.
But we, indeed, who call things good and fair,
The evil is upon us while we speak;
Deliver us from evil, let us pray.

How much better had all this been if written straight forward in clear prose utterance!

43.2

He ended. There was silence in the church;
We heard a baby sucking in its sleep
At the farthest end of the aisle. Then spoke a man,
'Now, look to it, coves, that all the beef and drink
Be not filched from us like the other fun;
For beer's spilt easier than a woman is!
This gentry is not honest with the poor;
They bring us up, to trick us.'—'Go it, Jim,'
A woman screamed back,—'I'm a tender soul;
I never banged a child at two years old
And drew blood from him, but I sobbed for it
Next moment,—and I've had a plague of seven.

you did?

43.3

Be sure I'm well, I'm merry, I'm at ease,
But such a long way, long way, long way off,
I think you'll find me sooner in my grave,
And that's my choice, observe. For what remains,
An over-generous friend will care for me,
And keep me happy . . happier . .
'There's a blot!
This ink runs thick . . we light girls lightly weep . . .
And keep me happier . . was the thing to say, . .
Than as your wife I could be!—O, my star,
My saint, my soul! for surely you're my soul,
Through whom God touched me! I am not so lost
I cannot thank you for the good you did,
The tears you stopped, which fell down bitterly,
Like these—the times you made me weep for joy

How extremely probable the story is getting!

3.4

They see, for mysteries, through the open doors,
Vague puffs of smoke from pots of earthenware;
And fain would enter, when their time shall come,
With quite a different body than St. Paul
Has promised,—husk and chaff, the whole barley-corn,
Or where's the resurrection?'
'Thus it is,'
I sighed. And he resumed with mournful face.
'Beginning so, and filling up with clay
The wards of this great key, the natural world,
And fumbling vainly therefore at the lock
Of the spiritual,—we feel ourselves shut in
With all the wild-beast roar of struggling life,
The terrors and compunctions of our souls,
As saints with lions,—we who are not saints,
And have no heavenly lordship in our stare
To awe them backward! Ay, we are forced, so pent,
To judge the whole too partially, . . confound
Conclusions. Is there any common phrase
Significant, when the adverb's heard alone,
The verb being absent, and the pronoun out?

The news from England, tho'? The news, then the sermon!—

43.5

He stood a moment with erected brows,
In silence, as a creature might, who gazed:
Stood calm, and fed his blind, majestic eyes
Upon the thought of perfect noon. And when
I saw his soul saw,—'Jasper first,' I said,
'And second, sapphire; third, chalcedony;
The rest in order, . . last, an amethyst.'

A very beautiful tempest in a teapot. What a gift of utterance this high child has,—and how very weak and childlike all it has to say.

THE END.

12 jan⁾, 1857—

44 George Grote, *Histoire de la Grèce depuis les Temps les Plus Reculés jusqu'à la Fin de la Generation Contemporaine d'Alexandre le Grand*
Paris: Librairie Internationale, 1864–67
233 × 147 mm

George Grote acquired a strong taste for Classics while a schoolboy at Charterhouse. Made to leave school and join his father's London bank in 1810, aged fifteen, he continued to read them avidly, along with German and political economy. He was involved in the circle of the Utilitarian James Mill, who was fascinated by Greek history and deeply aware of the political bias of William Mitford's *History of Greece* (1784–1810). Since at least early 1823, Grote had noted a scholarly lacuna, writing to his friend and fellow businessman George Warde Norman that January: 'I am at present deeply engaged in the fabulous ages of Greece, which I find will require to be illustrated by bringing together a large mass of analogical matter from other early histories, in order to show the entire uncertainty and worthlessness of tales to which early associations have so long familiarized all classical minds.' The philosopher John Stuart Mill records that Grote's *History* was begun 'at my father's instigation', although, according to Mrs Grote, the impetus came from her towards the autumn of 1823: 'You are always studying the ancient authors whenever you have a moment's leisure; now here would be a fine subject for you to treat. Suppose you try your hand!'

Grote's *History*, based on modern German scholarship and radical political principles, was finally published in ten volumes between 1846 and 1856, and was immediately recognised as the best Greek history in Europe. It was especially welcomed by the younger Mill, who was much influenced by it. Grote pioneered the separation of Greek myth from history and established the importance of Athenian democracy as a model for modern democratic reformers; he also defended the reputation of Athenian demagogues and sophists against the attacks of ancient authors. His work is still regarded as the foundation of modern research in Greek history.

Grote's *History of Greece* was translated into German (1850–56), Italian (1855–58) and at least partially into Russian (1860). The nineteen-volume French translation of 1864–67 was authorised by Grote and made from the second English edition by Dr A.-L. de Sadous of what was then the Lycée Imperial de Versailles. It has a specific index and errata list, albeit, unlike the German edition, no translator's preface. The plates have been transferred directly from the English, retaining English headings, place names and, confusingly, volume numbers; a list assisted French bookbinders to place the plates correctly.

This copy was Grote's own. It is one of only two copies in British libraries.

44.1

44.1 Harriet Grote, *The Personal Life of George Grote*, 2nd edn (London, 1873), frontispiece, showing George Grote

44.2 *Histoire de la Grèce*, vol. 16, plate detail, showing map of Syracuse

44.2

No.	NAME.	Age.	Residence.	Certificate.	College, &c.	Place of Birth.	Division.	REMARKS.

45.1

45   Examination registers

1838–89

472 × 345 mm; UoL/D1-D69

The sixty-six volumes of examination registers, 1838–89, represent one of the largest surviving records of the main activity of the University of London before 1900. This was the setting and regulation of examinations. During the nineteenth century the matriculation examination, roughly equivalent to a modern GCSE, developed from the entrance examination to the University into a more general qualification for various professions. By 1871, passing the matriculation examination was a means of gaining part or complete exemption from examinations for the Royal College of Surgeons, the Royal Military College at Sandhurst and some branches of the legal profession. The University of London, a pioneer in terms of examinations, awarded the first B.Sc. degrees in this country, and it was the first university in England to award degrees to women. The examination registers illustrate this, as well as recording candidates for a multiplicity of other types of degree. The University had a global presence by the second half of the nineteenth century: the colonial volume, 1869–87, includes the names of candidates from Mauritius, Canada, the West Indies and India.

The examination registers are huge, leather-bound volumes with handwritten entries, arranged by the centre at which the examinations took place. Many of these centres, such as Owens College in Manchester and University College, Bristol, later became independent universities. The volumes contain information that in some cases will be hard, if not impossible, to find elsewhere. For example, candidates' addresses were often noted in years that fell between censuses. Examinees were sometimes as local as Tottenham Court Road, Southampton Street (Strand) or Woburn Square, sometimes from further afield, such as Kent, Somerset, Cornwall or Scotland. Most registers contain at least seven facts about a candidate, such as his (and later her) full name, age, certificate (recording proof of birth or good conduct) and the place of study (often given as 'private study' or 'private tuition'). The beginning of the first volume included the names of the examiners in Classics, mathematics, chemistry and natural history. They were high-powered scholars, including William Thomas Brande for chemistry, Robert Murphy for mathematics, Connop Thirlwall (a friend of George Grote) for Classics and John Stevens Henslow for botany.

Even qualifying for an examination was an onerous task: a candidate for the Bachelor of Medicine degree in 1856 was obliged to supply no fewer than seven certificates. Among the luminaries whose details are listed in these volumes are Alexander Graham Bell, Walter Bagehot, and Sir William Schwenck Gilbert, of Gilbert and Sullivan fame.

45.1 detail of entries for June 1868, including the entry for Alexander Graham Bell

46 Manuscript designs by Walter Crane for Mary de Morgan, *The Necklace of Princess Fiorimonde and Other Stories*

c. 1877–80

Various sizes, mounted to 248 × 200 mm; SL.IV.67

46.1 design for cover

46.2 upper board, *The Necklace of Princess Fiorimonde* (London, 1880)

46.3 design for frontispiece

46.4 frontispiece

46.5 design for 'The Prince and the Wizard'

46.6 'The Prince and the Wizard'

The painter, illustrator, writer and designer Walter Crane (1845–1915) was a superb technician in all skills relating to the making of books, especially designing illustrations. Unlike many of his contemporaries, he seemed to know instinctively how to draw with the engraver in mind. His most celebrated illustrations are perhaps those made for a series of forty-one *Picture Books* for children, wood-engraved in colour by Edmund Evans and published almost exclusively by Routledge (1865–76). However, his black-and-white work, as revealed here and done in graphite (with the exception of the cover design, which is in watercolour), shows his typically strong line. The drawings are both vivacious and meticulous, again Crane hallmarks. Crane made a profound study of medieval illuminated books, incunabula and Japanese prints, as well as the paintings and book designs of the Pre-Raphaelites, and his designs here are stylistically elegant and redolent of an Arts and Crafts aestheticism and a remote world of medieval myth.

Of Mary de Morgan's three volumes of fairy tales, *The Necklace of Princess Fiorimonde and Other Stories* is the only one illustrated by Crane. There is a manuscript design for each of the twenty-nine illustrations in the printed book: cover, full-page illustrations, headpieces and initials, and tailpieces. With the exception of the cover, there is a clear correspondence between the design and print versions. Although the print occasionally loses elements present in the design – a setting sun or a bird on the back of an old man's neck – on the whole it tends to be more complete. Lines are added in the borders of tailpieces, there is more shading, and we see increased detail. For example, in the printed frontispiece a goldfish bowl contains fish, a pond sports more fish than in the drawing, Princess Fiorimonde's necklace has more links, the belt of her dress has a ruche below the sash, and her sleeves have two puffs. Occasionally the amendments are more striking. For instance, whereas the design for Princess Fiorimonde at her looking glass shows her standing, in the printed text she is kneeling, and a window and a vase of flowers have been added. A picture of Prince Michael and the wizard facing p. 87 of the printed text is a mirror image of the drawing.

Sir Louis Sterling purchased six sets of drawings by Crane between August 1930 and May 1938. Those for *Princess Fiorimonde* are the only ones for a published volume. Designs and book together cost him £18 in August 1931.

46.1

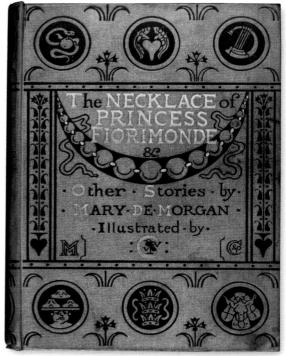

46.2

"She was in the garden, lying on the marble edge of a fountain, feeding the gold fish who swam in the water."—Frontispiece.

"'Tis their daughter, Princess Joan," said the wizard with a sigh. "But do not look at her, my son, for she will bring nothing but trouble to all who know her."—P. 87.

47 **Alfred, Lord Tennyson, manuscript of**
The Voyage of Maeldune
1879 or 1880
220 × 188 mm; SL.V.32

Alfred, Lord Tennyson's 'The Voyage of Maeldune', published in *Ballads, and Other Poems* (1880) and written during a period of resurgent creative energy, is an adaptation of a well-known Irish legend in P. W. Joyce's *Old Celtic Romances* (1879). The poem relates the adventures of a chieftain who seeks to avenge his father's death but who is blown off course on a Ulyssean voyage of enchantment and calamity. The journey brings him to magic islands that cast a frenzied spell on his crew, who fall to slaying each other. The spell is broken only on the Isle of a Saint, where they encounter a hermit who admonishes forgiveness. Weary of strife and sin, the mariners return home. On seeing his father's killer, the hero forsakes revenge and leaves him be.

Composed in 1879–80, the poem is written in black ink with extensive revisions in Tennyson's hand on thirteen leaves of ruled laid paper, with a watermark of a post-horn inside a crowned shield above a monogram formed of the letters 'JA' and the lettering 'JALLINS | SUPERFINE | 1879'. The pages were torn with hurried force from a copybook now held at the Houghton Library, Harvard (Harvard Notebook 47), which contains other early fragments of the poem.

The ragged, dirty pages, which show signs of having been rolled up at one point, seem a far cry from the poem's lush imagery and the rhythmical marvel of its anapaestic hexameter. But these 'chips of the workshop' are significant for what they reveal about Tennyson's methods of composition. They significantly modify the well-known story that Tennyson composed in his head while walking up and down the garden before committing his poem to paper.

The manuscript is a working document, containing the final stages of creation as Tennyson fair-copied and further revised the poem. The resulting text is, besides relatively small variants, identical to the published version, for which the manuscript likely served as printer's copy. Comparison with the first draft, found in Harvard Notebook 64, shows that Tennyson did not write his stanzas in the order of the finished poem.

47.1

When he had fashioned and refined the fragmentary stanzas in that Notebook, producing their final version, he removed the pages and numbered them from 99 to 106 in blue pencil. This fixed the poem's final sequence and determined its position in the volume, an act that represents in effect the last stage in Tennyson's poetic imagination.

This is one of six Tennyson autograph manuscripts and revised proof sheets in the Sterling Library. Sir Louis Sterling purchased it *c.* 1931–32, together with that of 'Early Spring', for £300, presumably from the London bookseller C. J. Sawyer. Sawyer had bought the two manuscripts from Sotheby's on 7 July 1930. Both had been part of a group of twelve sold at auction by C. B. L. Tennyson CMG, the laureate's grandson, 'by order of the tenant for life' and 'pursuant to the authority of the Court' (*The Times*, 8 July 1930).

47.1 fol. 1

47.2 fol. 2

47.3 fol. 3

47.4 fol. 3a

47.5 fol. 4

And we came to the Silent Isle that we never had touch'd at before
Where a silent Ocean always broke on a silent shore,
And the hooks glitter'd on in the light without sound & the long water-falls
Pour'd in a thunderless plunge to the base of the mountain walls,
And the poplar & cypress unshaken by storm flourish'd up beyond sight,
And the pine shot aloft from the crag to an unbelievable height,
And high in the heaven above it there flicker'd a songless lark,
And the cock couldn't crow & the bull couldn't low & the dog couldn't bark.
And round it we went & thro' it, but never a murmur, a breath—
It was all of it fair as life, but all of it quiet as death.
And we hated the beautiful Isle, for whenever we strove to speak
Our voices were thinner & fainter than any flittermouse-shriek
And they that were mighty of tongue & could raise such a battle-cry
That a hundred who heard it would rush on a thousand lances & die—
O they to be dumb'd by the charm!—so fill'd with their anger were they
They almost fell on each other but after we sail'd away

And we came to the Isle of Shouting where up a rosen wild bird
cried from the topmost summit with human voices & words
... in an hour they cried, & whenever their voices peal'd
The stars fell down at the plot & the harvest died from the field
And the men dropt dead in the vallies & half of the cattle went lame,
And the roof sank in on the hearth, & the house broke into flame;
And the shouting of those wild birds ran into the hearts of my crew
... they fought one another & slew.
But I drew them from the other. I saw that we could not stay
And we left the dead to the birds & we sail'd with our wounded away

Till they shouted along with the shouting & seized on one another & slew;

And the cloven ... from the cliffs, & the white-faced jessamine, ...
And gay with ... blossom the long convolvulus hung;

And each was a cricket, with ... in the middle-day heat.
Dolphin & ...

And we came to the Isle of Flowers, ...
In ... & the middle summer sat ... on the lap of the breeze,
And the ... passion-flower to the cliffs, & the ...
And stood with a myriad blossom the long convolvulus hung;
And the topmost peak of the mountain was lilies in lieu of snow,
And the lilies like glaciers winded down, running out below
Thro' the fire of ... & poppies, the blaze of gorse, & the blush
Of millions of roses that sprang without leaf on a thorn from the bush
And the whole isle-side flashing down from the summit with never a tree
Swept like a torrent of gems from the sky to the blue of the sea
And we roll'd upon capes of crocus & gambol'd our fill & we ...
And we wallow'd in beds of lilies, & chanted the triumph of Finn
And each like a golden image was pollen'd from head to feet
... at length ... away & languid & ...
... & ... of blossom ...
And we hated the beautiful Isle, ... we hated the isle ...
And we tore up the flowers by the million & flung them in ...
And we left but a naked rock, & in anger we sail'd away

48 Degree certificate for Fanny McRae
1884

447 × 334 mm; UoL/AC/2/1/76

In 1878 the University of London became the first university in the United Kingdom to admit women to its honours degree examinations on the same terms as men.

As the University was instituted purely as an examining body, its students were not required to be resident, and so women could be admitted without being impeded by the strictures of Victorian social and moral convention. Indeed, it was the distinctions drawn by the University between residence and teaching, and between teaching and presentation for examinations, that helped facilitate women's degrees before they could have been possible within the traditional Oxbridge model.

48.1

However, the road to female parity had been a long one, with the campaign stretching back to the 1860s. Although in 1862 the then Vice-Chancellor of the University, George Grote, stated that admission of women to degrees was required 'by the plainest principles of justice', it was over a decade before the University Senate agreed. During this time the University's Convocation passed three resolutions in favour. At the heated debate of January 1876 it was stressed that women should not be restricted to taking general examinations that covered similar ground to honours papers but led to no degree award, as 'where a woman had fairly earned a reward she should not be deprived of it'.

Such was the strength of feeling on this occasion that the motion to allow admittance to degrees was carried for all subjects, and not just the arts, which had been the original premise. In 1877 the University Senate voted for a supplementary charter permitting the conferment of medical degrees on women, despite opposition from a group of medical graduates who petitioned against the innovation. Once this had been carried, the admittance of women to all degrees in all faculties swiftly followed, and the charter decreeing this was obtained in 1878. The first women students graduated in 1880, when four passed the BA examination. In the following year two women were awarded a B.Sc.

Although the custom is for the graduate student to keep his or her degree certificate, a representative sample can be found in the University Archive. The earliest degree certificate retained for a woman graduate is that of Fanny McRae (AC 2/1/76), who obtained Honours in Classics at the examination for the degree of BA in 1884 – the same year in which Sophie Bryant was the first woman to be awarded a D.Sc. from the University. The Senate minutes for 1884 reveal that Fanny obtained her degree by 'private study and tuition', a common route for many women who had neither the money nor the time to attend formal classes, although others were able to take advantage of the classes offered by the Birkbeck Institute (open to women since 1830) and at University College, which led the way in offering mixed-sex classes to its students from 1878.

In the year in which Fanny McRae took her degree, she was one of thirteen women (11.4 per cent of candidates) in the first division and seventeen women in total (9.7 per cent of candidates) to take a degree. By 1900 the proportion of female graduates had increased to 30 per cent. The University's commitment to degrees for women helped to break down the notion of 'separate spheres' for the sexes and ensured that it led in the advancement of teaching and learning and the breakdown of inequality in higher education.

48.1 degree certificate for Fanny McRae

48.2 UoL /CH/10/2/2, interior of a room at College Hall, the University of London's first women's hall of residence, *c.* 1900

48.3 UoL/CH/10/1/16, the early London graduate Louisa MacDonald (1858–1949), BA, Hons I (1884); MA (1886)

48.4 UoL/CH/10/1/16, the archaeologist Mary Brodrick (1858–1933; University College London 1890–1906)

48.2

48.3

48.4

Author of 'Honor Bright', *Halt!*
London: Wells Gardner, Darton & Co., 1893
188 × 121 mm

As a completely unknown work, *Halt!* carries no publicly acknowledged critical status. A degree of murk surrounds its very authorship, firstly because 'the Author of "Honor Bright"', to whom it is attributed, has not been traced, and secondly because *Honor Bright* (1879) emanates from more than one hand. The assumption must be that 'the authors of "The Two Sparrows", "Robin and Linnet" ' who feature on *Honor Bright*'s title-page were reduced to only one by the time of *Halt!*'s publication in 1893. The anonymous illustrator was Arthur G. Walker (1861–1939), better known as a sculptor and painter.

What distinguishes the book's place within the dozen or so companion volumes by its author(s) is that this is currently the only copy recorded in an institutional library. The authors of *Honor Bright* have worked within the genre of the Victorian family story (*Honor Bright* being a modest secularisation of Charlotte Yongery as found in Yonge's *The Daisy Chain* of 1856, while *Halt!* belongs to a run of stories that feature the brothers Tom and Bertie). *Halt!* draws its title and its message from a perception that it would be wise of the young to obey those of a larger experience and understanding, as the marching soldier must obey his commanding officer. This is not too overdone, and the occasional references to a Higher Power, with appropriate scriptural quotations, are no more than is expected of the stories of the period.

The book was donated to the University of London by Dr J. H. P. Pafford, one-time Goldsmiths' Librarian at Senate House. It is part of a collection that he garnered during his many raids on the nation's second-hand and antiquarian bookshops, buying books sporting reward labels that bore witness to ornamental typographic styling, to the location and character of the awarding institution and to the name and achievement of the recipient. The elaborate, non-denominational label in *Halt!* records the book's gift to Frederick Coleman at Winfrith Church Sunday School in December 1895. We are not told the reason; perhaps regular attendance throughout the year, perhaps merely a Christmas present.

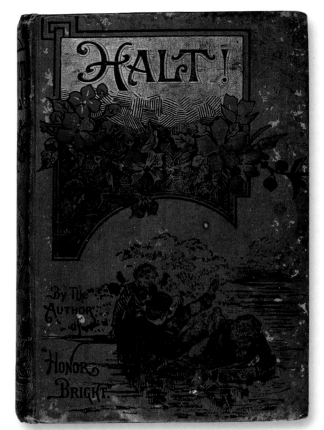

49.1

" One second she was there, . . . and then she was gone."—*See page 8o.*

49.2

49.1 upper board

49.2 plate facing p. 76, 'One second she was there, … and then she was gone'

50 *Aglaia*

1893–94

309 × 244 mm

In 1890 the stained-glass designer Henry Holiday (1839–1927) heard a debate on dress reform by the Healthy & Artistic Dress Union at Hampstead Town Hall. Holiday was inspired to join and quickly became a prime mover, joining a roster of élite Vice-Presidents that included artists and physicians, and eventually becoming President. As he recorded in *Reminiscences of my Life* (*c*. 1914), Holiday believed that the Union's work would be ineffective without a journal. Thus *Aglaia* was established in 1893, with Holiday as editor, the major contributor and an illustrator.

The journal existed 'to inculcate sound principles [for] devising and executing beautiful and healthy garments'. Articles focused on healthy and artistic aspects of modern dress, ranging from 'Corset wearing' and 'Cycling costume' to 'The walking dress'. Emphasis on grace and beauty linked the Union to the ideals of the Arts and Crafts movement. Contributors included the painter G. F. Watts, Sophie Bryant (the first woman recipient of a D.Sc. from the University of London), Walter Crane and Arthur Lasenby Liberty (1843–1917), founder of the Liberty Company, who wrote an article on the progress of taste in dress in relation to manufacture. There would be no 'fear of singularity', as: 'if the suggestions made in this Journal are wise in themselves, and are felt to be so by any considerable number of persons, it follows that those who adopt them […] will not be chargeable with personal eccentricity.' Walter Crane broadened the debate in the third and final issue on the progress of taste in dress relating to art education.

Only three issues of *Aglaia* were produced, at irregular intervals between July 1893 and autumn 1894, circulated to members and sold for one shilling per issue. Holiday wrote that 'the writing was very onerous work for myself' and that *Aglaia* was not viable, as railway bookstalls would not stock a publication that appeared less than quarterly. The Union published another journal, *The Dress Review*, between approximately 1902 and 1906, but once again this was short-lived. For comparison, the *Rational Dress Society's Gazette* (1888–89), which also looked at health, beauty and practical ways to achieve rational dress, ceased to publish after only six issues.

Aglaia is now scarce, with complete copies known in just three British institutional repositories.

50.1 issue 1, title-page

50.2 detail of issue 2, p. 42, line drawings of walking dresses

50.1

50.2

51 Walter de la Mare, *Peacock Pie: A Book of Rhymes*

London: Constable, 1921 (annotated 7th impression of 1913 edn)
228 × 148 mm; with proofs for 1924 edn, 254 × 159 mm

Peacock Pie is Walter de la Mare's best-known and best-loved collection of poems for children. It has been continuously in print for almost a century, and nearly three-quarters of the poems have been set to music, 'Silver' as many as twenty-nine times. It marks a turning point in its author's career, as he subsequently concentrated on writing poems for adults.

Five distinct new editions of the book, with five different artists, appeared during de la Mare's lifetime, between 1916 and 1946, as well as reprints of the original, unillustrated version. De la Mare had intended the original 1913 edition to include pictures too, and had arranged in 1912 for a brilliant young artist, Claud Lovat Fraser, to produce some coloured 'embellishments', but the publisher, Constable, considered their reproduction too expensive. It is these illustrations that de la Mare added in the 1924 edition, via the marked-up reprint from 1921 and two sets of proofs, and so eventually achieved his ambition. Among *Peacock Pie* illustrations, only Edward Ardizzone's from 1946 surpass these sixteen in artistic quality.

Peacock Pie

51.2

20 PEACOCK PIE

THE SHIP OF RIO

THERE was a ship of Rio
  Sailed out into the blue,
And nine and ninety monkeys
  Were all her jovial crew.
From bo'sun to the cabin boy,
  From quarter to caboose,
There weren't a stitch of calico
  To breech 'em—tight or loose;
From spar to deck, from deck to keel,
  From barnacle to shroud,
There weren't one pair of reach-me-downs
  To all that jabbering crowd.
But wasn't it a gladsome sight,
  When roared the deep-sea gales,
To see them reef her fore and aft,
  A-swinging by their tails!
Oh, wasn't it a gladsome sight,
  When glassy calm did come,
To see them squatting tailor-wise
  Around a keg of rum!
Oh, wasn't it a gladsome sight,
  When in she sailed to land,
To see them all a-scampering skip
  For nuts across the sand!

51.1

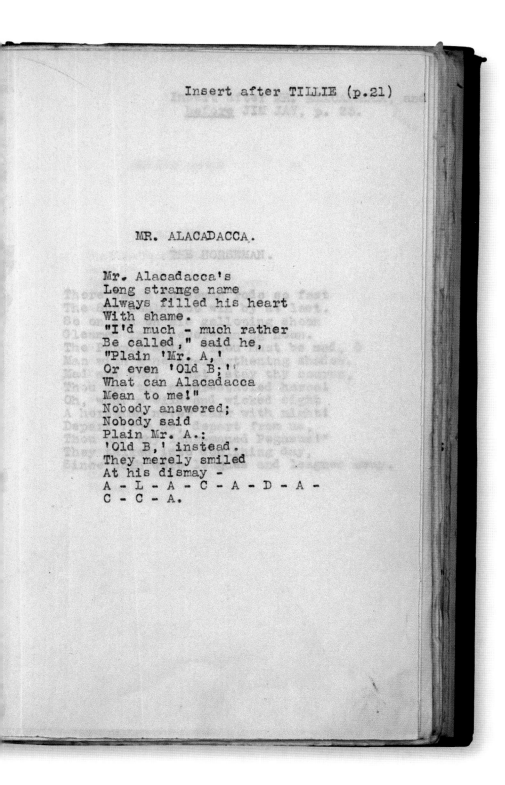

The marked-up text from 1921 contains tipped-in typescripts of nine out of the ten new poems that were added in the 1924 edition. A tenth new poem, 'Polly Pie', is also included as a typescript. It is printed but crossed out in the first proofs, to appear in revised form as 'A – Apple Pie' in *Bells and Grass* (1941). Another new poem, 'Snow', replaced it in the second proofs. The sixteen new illustrations in the 1924 edition were listed in pencil in the first proofs and in print in the second proofs, which included colour proofs of them all.

Some of the new poems underwent substantial revision in the proofs. Only four of them – 'Not I!', 'Snow', 'Blind Tam' (later called 'The Penny Owing') and 'Groat nor Tester' – reappeared in *Collected Rhymes and Verses* (1944). The six others came back into print in the *Complete Poems* and in the definitive edition of *Peacock Pie* (both 1969). The 1924 edition is significant for being the only one ever to contain extra poems. The three illustrated poems among them – 'Mr Alacadacca', 'Must and May' and 'Late' – must have been written by 1912, when, according to de la Mare, Lovat Fraser did all the illustrations. As de la Mare describes the additional poems in the 1924 edition as 'new-old', he may have written at least six of the others by then too. The edition was never reprinted.

Mr Alacadacca

51.1 1921 issue, copy marked up for new edition, with inserted typescript, 'Mr. Alacadacca'

51.2 proof drawing, 'Peacock Pie'

51.3 proof drawing, 'Mr. Alacadacca'

51.3

Rich Past All Belief

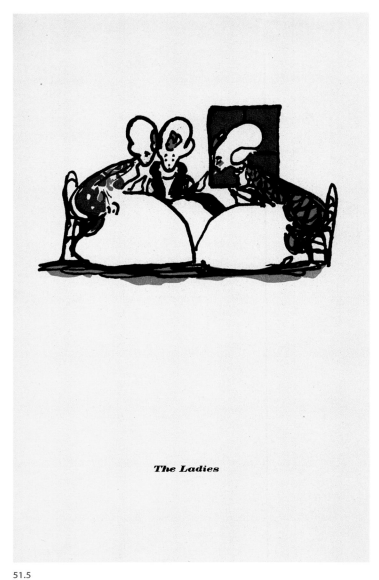

The Ladies

51.4

51.5

51.4 proof drawing, 'Rich Past All Belief'

51.5 proof drawing, 'The Ladies'

51.6 proof drawing, 'Late'

51.7 proof drawing, 'Oughtoo'

Late

51.6

Oughtoo

51.7

52 Designs by Thomas Sturge Moore for books by W. B. Yeats

Design 185 × 115 mm, book 197 × 130 mm;
MS978/3/2/35

The Irish poet (and Bloomsbury resident) W. B. Yeats had known and collaborated with the Hampstead poet and artist Thomas Sturge Moore since the 1890s. It was while Sturge Moore was designing the cover for Yeats's *Responsibilities and Other Poems*, the companion volume to *Reveries over Childhood and Youth*, that Yeats asked him to provide a new visual identity, a cover design of 'great beauty […] better suited for my American books in general than the design for "Reveries"'. Yeats hoped, too, that Macmillan London would also use it (though not for all of his books). He concluded that 'the block should be made in London & that the expense of this will not fall on me'.

Sturge Moore offered his panelled design of a stylised rose and thorns. As Yeats paid £14 13*s*. 10*d*. 'to settle account', he returned the 'excellent' design, suggesting that Sturge Moore

do it all in the same thin lines – rose and all. This is merely a suggestion – have thick lines for the Rose if you will. I have a notion that the rose will look more unusual in the same thin lines as the rest – it is itself a convention that one knows & yet so simply that it could hardly be changed. I think it a fine grave design.

Sturge Moore's symbolic rose first appeared on *Per Amica Silentia Lunae* (1917). It offered W. B. Yeats the chance to reappear under an older iconography and to forestall anonymous American book designers chosen by the Macmillan Company of New York and whose work he much disliked. The rose had had only a diminished presence in Yeats's work after 1912, and is not used within the text of *Per Amica*. In the cover design for *The Cutting of an Agate* (1919) the rose of *Per Amica* morphs into a mask, the dominant symbol of both books. But the rose design is also used on the American (but not the English) edition of *The Wild Swans at Coole* (1919) and on one issue of the American *Selected Poems* (1921). Sturge Moore had even provided for spines of different thicknesses, offering one spinal design of a single thorned stem, and another of a pair of such stems. Sturge Moore's book covers were eventually to become a visual encyclopaedia of Yeats's leading symbols.

52.1 W. B. Yeats, *Per Amica Silentia Lunae* (London, 1918), upper board, designed by T. Sturge Moore

52.2 MS978/3/3/2, bookplate for W. B. Yeats, designed by T. Sturge Moore

52.3 MS978/3/3/2, bookplate for W. B. Yeats's wife, George, designed by T. Sturge Moore

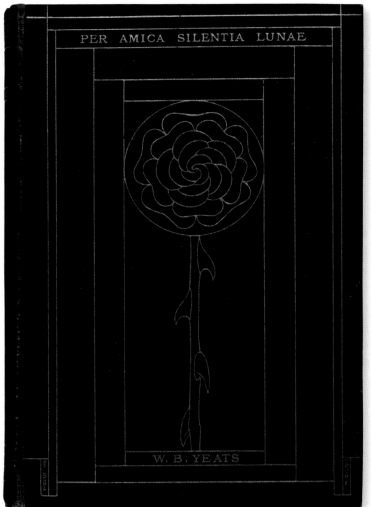

52.1

52.2

52.3

53 Manuscript letter from Sir Arthur Conan Doyle
to Harry Price
22 February [1928]
203 × 127 mm; HPC/4B/55D

The parapsychologist Harry Price first came to
prominence in 1922 for exposing the spirit photographer William Hope of the 'Crewe Circle', who produced
portraits for sitters that featured ghostly 'extras', or
likenesses, of their departed loved ones. Supported by
the Society of Psychical Research (SPR), he arranged to
have a séance with Hope, to whom he gave discreetly
pinpricked dark slides and photographic plates which
had been exposed by x-ray with the manufacturer's lion
rampant trademark. When it became apparent that
Hope switched the marked plates with his own, Price
declared him a fraud. He published his findings in the
SPR *Journal*, and shortly afterwards reprinted them in
the sixpenny pamphlet *Cold Light on Spiritualist
'Phenomena'*.

Among those most eager to defend Hope was Sir
Arthur Conan Doyle (1859–1930), the leading spokes-
man of the worldwide Spiritualist movement then in
its heyday. 'The Hope case is more intricate than any
Holmes case I ever invented', he told the American
magician Harry Houdini. Although impressed by
Price's abilities as a psychical researcher, Doyle grew
anxious over his success in debunking several high-
profile mediums. He began an earnest correspondence
with Price in October 1922, as he drafted a vigorous
refutation of Price's experiment in *The Case for Spirit
Photography*; in private, he urged him to withdraw the
Hope pamphlet from circulation.

Over time, the once cordial relationship between
the two men became strained. In this letter Doyle
questions Price's professed impartiality in his para-
psychical experiments with Hope, Mrs Deane and the
well-known Cottingley fairy photographs: 'It is all very
well to say that you are not "anti-spiritualist" but your
record is all the other way.' The irreparable break
occurred when Doyle learned that Price repeated an
embarrassing anecdote involving Doyle and two
fraudulent mediums from New York who had
'materialized' his deceased mother. In retaliation Doyle
angrily threatened to evict Price from space he rented
from the London Spiritual Alliance. Doyle's death in
1930 prevented their reconciliation, but Price would
later reflect, 'Poor, dear, lovable, credulous Doyle! He
was a giant in stature with the heart of a child.'

53.1 letter, p. 1.

53.2 Harry Price, *Cold Light on Spiritualistic
'Phenomena'* (London, 1922), front wrapper

53.3 HPG/1/II/1(ii), alleged spirit photograph
by William Hope, 1922 (sitter: Harry Price)

53.1

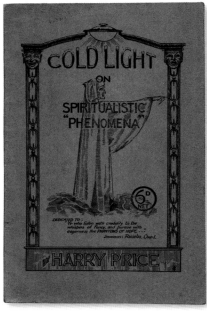

53.2

53.3

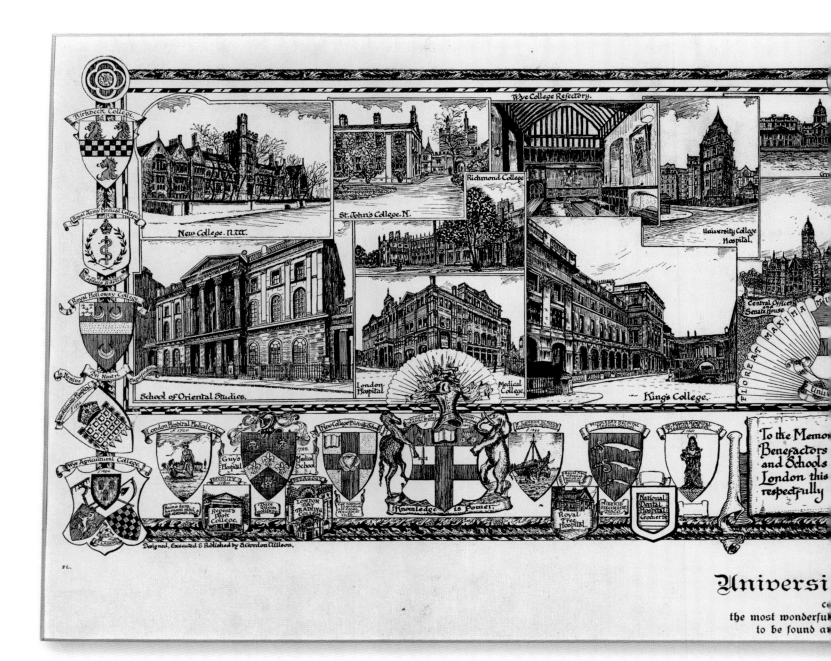

54 **S. Gordon Wilson, Picture of the aggregate Colleges**
1923
557 × 217 mm, mounted to 699 × 376 mm;
UoL/ULC/PC/27/22

This picture portrays the federated University of London through a patchwork of twenty-two small sketches of the major colleges and schools, bordered on three sides by thirty coats of arms, one for each member institution.

The picture's creator was the historian and vicar Stanley Gordon Wilson, who wrote that the opportunity to prepare it resulted from a motorcycling accident. A reduced version (138 × 417 mm) appears as the frontispiece of his *The University of London and its*

Colleges (1923), which claimed to be the first illustrated account of the University of London ever published. Internal evidence shores the picture firmly in its time: not only by the inclusion of the School of Tropical Medicine, which joined the University in 1924, but also by the omission of the School of Pharmacy, which joined in 1925, and the individual status accorded to New College and Hackney College, united in 1924 by an Act of Parliament. Since then, the university has again changed considerably, now comprising nineteen institutions. Many member institutions have merged. Others, such as Wye College and New College, have closed down. Institutions have also joined, such as the Courtauld Institute (1932), London Business School (1964) and the Institute of Cancer Research (2003).

of London

ng
tion of institutions
in the World.

54.1

As a representation of the aggregate Colleges, with variety of architectural forms and individual crests, the picture entrenches a sense of multiplicity. However, taking centre stage are the words 'Floreat maxima mundi totius universitas' ('The greatest university in the whole world flourishes'), which emphasise the Colleges' greater unity as a combined whole. This is precisely the message the artist wished to convey, writing: 'I send it [the book] forth trusting that it may help to foster the University Spirit which should be greater than Collegiate *esprit de corps*.' For Sir Sydney Russell-Wells, Member of Parliament for the University of London at the time, it answered the question sometimes heard: 'What and where is the University of London?'

54.1 picture of the aggregate colleges

54.2 UoL/RC/13/4/a, sample of University colours, 1907, with ribbon sample attached

54.2

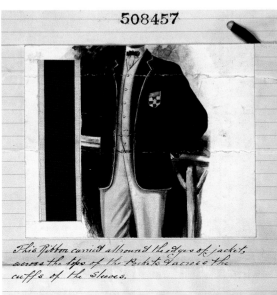

508457

This Ribbon carried all round the edges of jacket, across the tops of the Pockets & across the cuffs of the Sleeves.

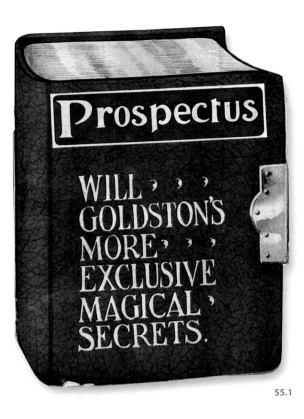

55.1

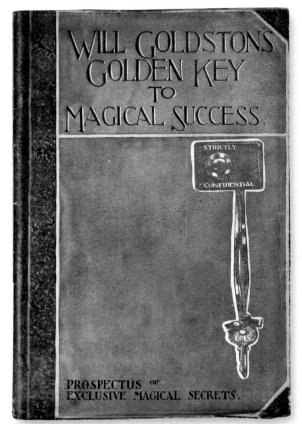

55.2

 55

Will Goldston, *More Exclusive Magical Secrets*
London: W. Goldston Ltd, 1921
253 × 186 mm

Will Goldston (1877–1948) made a name for himself in the first half of the twentieth century as a purveyor of magical goods, editor of magical magazines and, most notably, the author of a series of popular books explaining the secrets of conjuring and magic. The most celebrated, and still the most sought after, of these were the three volumes of his *Exclusive Magical Secrets*, produced between 1912 and 1927. These books targeted the conjuring fraternity, offering to put into their hands the secrets of the most celebrated and mystifying tricks and illusions. *More Exclusive Magical Secrets* (1921) was produced in a limited de luxe edition of 750 numbered copies, each bound in red sheepskin and costing 4 guineas. The numbers available to different areas of the world were tantalisingly rationed: 250 each to Britain and the USA, 100 to India and a mere 10 to New Zealand. The book was furnished with a substantial brass lock, 'of such strange device that no one (save Houdini or a professional burglar) will be able to pick it', and Goldston required every subscriber to sign an undertaking not to reveal anything of its contents to outsiders. Magic and money are interwined at every level in Goldston's marketing

of his books. 'When [the owner] is not actually using the book himself,' urged Goldston, 'he will lock it up from others just as he locks up his cash box', hinting that the book will indeed be a cash box for the aspiring magician.

More Exclusive Magical Secrets contains sections on 'pocket tricks', 'small apparatus tricks', 'platform and stage tricks', 'Chinese tricks' and 'automata and ventriloquial' devices. The prospectus to *Exclusive Magical Secrets* promised that all the volumes would be issued on the same day 'so that in this respect no subscriber will have any advantage over another'. However, the first copy of *More Exclusive Magical Secrets* contains on its title-page the following dedication to its recipient: 'Congratulations to friend Harry Price. You possess the 1st copy many hours before other subscribers receive their copies. Best wishes. Sincerely yours Will Goldston November 1921.' Given this inscription, the most interesting section is that dealing with 'anti-spiritualistic tricks', which includes 'The Crystal Evulgograph' ('writing-revealer') invented by Price himself, to enable the reading of questions supposedly placed in sealed envelopes and burned. *More Exclusive Magical Secrets* is perhaps a microcosm of the Harry Price Library, occupying, as it does, the middle ground between secrecy and exposure, credulity and knowingness, magic and rationality.

black leather of the same material as his boots. This stirrup should be drawn upwards and placed into pocket by performer unseen.

The Crystal "Evulgograph."

FROM LATIN *Evulgo*; TO REVEAL, *graph*; WRITING.
INVENTED BY

HARRY PRICE, F.R.N.S.

Here is a novelty which will appeal to "thought-readers" who wish to mystify their audiences, both stage and drawing-room, as the apparatus can be used successfully at very close quarters.

The performer sends down slips of paper and envelopes with the request that the recipients of same write down any questions they please, fold the papers up themselves,

The Floating Skull.

The performer walks on to the stage with a skull in his hands. He slowly removes his hands, and the skull floats in the air. The performer passes a hoop over the skull and gives the hoop out for examination. The skull follows the conjurer round the stage and slowly sinks down again; the performer takes it in his hands, and retires.

The "skull" is really a balloon, made of silk covered

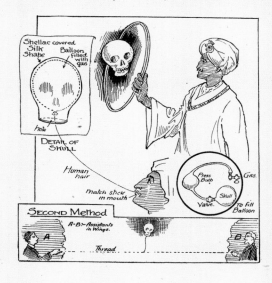

which is then screwed and roped up. The performer escapes very quickly.

The illustrations show the working of the case. The edges of the case are bound, and the trick is in the binding. All the screws, with the exception of two, are dummies, and therefore the removal of two screws

To get ready for her appearance the lady merely has to open the trap in the upper floor of the box and step through it. When she has done this the rubber cables draw the lower floor up against the upper floor, and when the box is removed from the stands the two floors are close together, and therefore there does not seem to be any place in the box in which the lady could have been concealed.

The top of the stand is ornamented with a fillet in order that it may appear to be narrower than it really is;

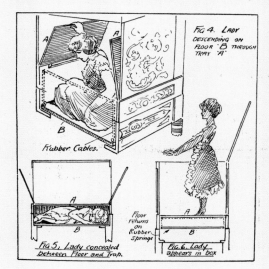

56 *The Fables of Esope*, illustrated by Agnes Miller Parker
Newtown, Montgomeryshire: Gregynog Press, 1931
306 × 216 mm

The 'Gregynog Aesop' is the twentieth of forty-five books issued between 1923 and 1940 by the private press established by the sisters Gwendoline and Margaret Davies at their house, Gregynog, near Newtown, Montgomeryshire. It is the Press's only issue of a work by Caxton, published without any editorial intervention. At this time the Controller of the Press was the Scottish painter William McCance, working with Blair Hughes-Stanton, but the quality of the printing really depended on Herbert Hodgson, who had earlier printed *The Seven Pillars of Wisdom*, and Richard Owen Jones, a skilled compositor from a local newspaper.

56.1

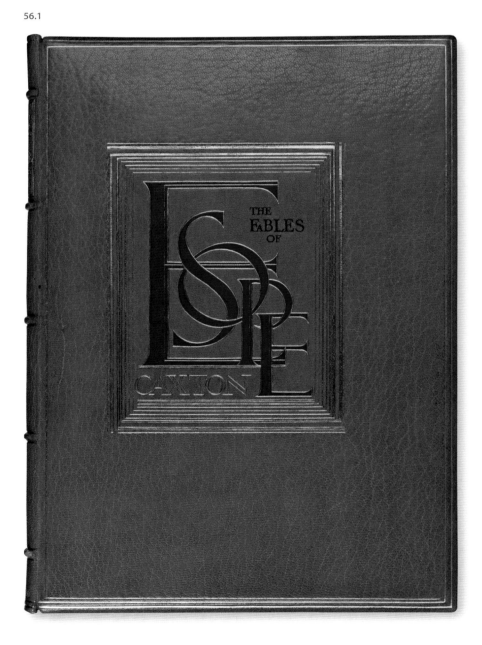

The text of the *Esope* was set, in Bembo, to perfection, and the presswork, on a Victoria platen, quite faultless. The paper used was a special making of Maidstone from Barcham Green, lightly sized, and damped before printing so that the finest lines of the illustrations could be shown to advantage. This was the first of two books illustrated by Agnes Miller Parker for the Gregynog Press. Her engravings have a brilliance of movement that ensnares the eye, with shading that darkens across the image towards small areas of solid black. Their depth of colour varies in strength, and in the darkest Hodgson added some white to the ink to lessen the contrast with the type. The large engraved initials by McCance, nearly twenty of them, an inch and three-quarters high, are more evenly cut, though less fluid in style. There is some crowding of the engravings by the closeness of the text matter, following a style that William Morris, founder of the private press movement, seems himself to have taken from the *Hypnerotomachia* of 1499, or from older manuscripts. Nonetheless, the University Printer at Cambridge, Walter Lewis, was to write to Dr Thomas Jones, Adviser to the Press, about the overall result, 'I do not think I have ever seen such a beautifully printed book', while the typographer Stanley Morison wrote to McCance, 'Nothing I could say would do justice to the excellence of every detail of the book.'

Books were bound at the press, and a small number of them were specially bound, usually by George Fisher. This copy is no. 16 of twenty-five copies specially bound by Fisher to a design by McCance of intertwining letters within gilt rules, which does not match in vitality those made to the more abstract designs of Blair Hughes-Stanton.

This copy is part of a complete set of the specially bound volumes from the Gregynog Press given to the Library in 1965 by Professor Sir David Hughes Parry, Chairman of the University Court between 1962 and 1970 and himself a Welshman.

56.1 upper board, showing William McCance's design of intertwining letters

56.2 p. 75, 'The horse, the hunter and the herte'

and we ſhalle chace the herte: and thow ſhalt hytte hym with thy ſwerd: and kyllė hym: and ſhalt take hym: and thenne his fleſſhe thow mayſt ete: and his ſkynne thow mayſt ſelle:

℃. And thenne the hunter moued by auaryce: demaunded of the hors: thynkeſt thow by thy feythe that we may take the herte: of whomme thow ſpekeſt to me of: ℃. And the hors anſwerd thus: Suffyſe the: For ther to I ſhalle put al my dylygence and alle my ſtrengthe: lepe vpon me: and doo after my counceylle: ℃. And thenne the Hunter lepte forthwith vpon the hors backe: And the hors beganne to renne after the herte: And whanne the herte ſawe: hym come he fled: And by cauſe that the hert ranne faſter: than the hors did: he ſcaped fro them:

56.3 detail of p. 49, 'The seuenth fable of the herte and of the hunter'

56.4 detail of p. 53, 'The yong man and the comyn woman'

56.5 detail of p. 82, 'The ant and the sygale'

56.6 detail of p. 132, initial O

56.7 detail of p. 133, initial N

56.8 detail of p. 2, initial H

56.3

56.4

THE XVIJ FABLE is of the ANT and of the SYGALE

56.5

F
th
fal
an
w
C
&
th

he fayd with a hyghe voy
and fowled my water: w
lord fauf your grece: Fo
me: Thenne fayd the wulf
drede to curfe me: And

56.6

ON
tha
oth
fab
tyr
har
age
anc

tooke hym in her kepynge
the wefel foo lytyl: he def
hare: wherof the wefel wa
wente: and beheld the Egle
And whanne fhe fawe hit

56.7

E
oug
or
hy
&
anc
to
dro

come vpward ageyne: the
my frend yf thow wylt hel
of this welle: For yf thov
walle: I fhal wel lepe vpon
I fhal lepe oute of this welle

56.8

57 Manuscript scores of Sir Arnold Bax, *A Lyke-Wake: Border Ballad*

1934

360 × 260 mm; MS435

Sir Arnold Bax (1883–1953) first wrote 'A Lyke-Wake' in 1908, for voice and piano. He orchestrated it much later, in 1934, but it was never performed in his lifetime. Bax notes in the manuscript that the original text is a 'border ballad'. In fact, it is generally believed to originate from North Yorkshire, and is particularly macabre.

'Lyke', based on the Old English *líc*, is an obsolete word for 'corpse', and is related to the German *Leiche*, of the same meaning. The wake is better known in modern practice, but traditionally served the specific purpose of allowing the soul time to depart from the deceased body. It is this period of time for which the ballad is intended, as the text is a warning to the living to care for the poor, and also to the soul as it journeys towards either heaven or hell.

The song is often referred to by its refrain, 'this ae night', and is perhaps more famously also used in Benjamin Britten's Serenade for Tenor, Horn and Strings (1943). Bax's version is violent in harmonic texture, and indeed sounds more overtly threatening than the ethereal and tense version by Britten. Bax was a man of independent means, a fine pianist and also a successful author. His artistic influences were dominated by Celtic mythology, especially that of Ireland, but in this work a curious kind of Englishness can be heard too. The opening passages evoke a slow death march, and the piece finally drifts away, following a furious crescendo which represents the fires of purgatory consuming the souls of those who had not provided charity to the poor. This is all written in Bax's trademark elegant and flowing notation.

In the last page of the work (pictured) it is clear that Bax is using an unusual version of the phrase 'fire and sleet', more commonly agreed as 'fire and fleet'. This is a reference to the warmth and comforts of home and what the soul has to leave in order to brave the journey either to Christ or to damnation, 'fleet' meaning 'floor' in Yorkshire dialect.

The autograph manuscript contains the versions both for voice and piano and for orchestra. It came to Senate House in 1955 from the pianist Harriet Cohen (1895–1967), together with twenty-seven scores, mainly of orchestral works, from Bax's library.

57.1 detail of p. 15, orchestral score

57.1

The 'Nazi Black Book' for Great Britain
1939
209 × 171 mm

The 'Nazi Black Book' for Great Britain is a photostatic reproduction and enlargement from US Army microfilm of the *Sonderfahndungsliste G. B.* Compiled by the *Einsatzgruppen*, it is similar to the one prepared in advance of Germany's invasion of Poland (*Sonderfahndungsbuch Polen*).

The volume begins with a booklet entitled *Fahndungsliste G. B.* ('Wanted List Great Britain'), naming individuals who were to be detained following the planned Operation Sea Lion in 1940. A pamphlet follows, listing major British firms such as Unilever and Lloyds of London, with brief details of their organisational structure and major officers, and German firms partly or wholly in British hands. Attached to the pamphlet is a further alphabetical list of towns, with their well-known institutions and firms that might be of use to occupiers, and inhabitants whose arrest was desired, cross-referenced to relevant pages of the *Fahndungsliste G. B.* booklet. Also listed were institutions that Nazis held in 'disfavour': unsurprisingly, anti-fascist organisations such as the British Non-Sectarian Anti-Nazi Committee and left-wing publishers, but also organisations as diverse as the Young Men's Christian Associations (YMCA) and Barclays Bank.

The nearly 3,000 people to be detained were a mixture of prominent British figures and notable non-British residents. The list was inaccurate because it contained the names of people who had recently died (for example, Sigmund Freud) or who had left the UK (the black American singer Paul Robeson). It was, nevertheless, thorough, listing nearly all prominent British politicians (including Neville Chamberlain) and their addresses. Also to be arrested were prominent individuals like Lord Baden-Powell, the founder of the Boy Scouts Movement (regarded as a spying organisation), Nancy Astor, Noel Coward and Virginia and Leonard Woolf. Wealthy Jews were on the list, such as the senior members of the Rothschild family. So were representatives of governments in exile, like Jan Masaryk and Edvard Beneš of Czechoslovakia. Most people listed were to go into the custody of *Amt IV* – the Gestapo.

The book's meticulous detail indicates the seriousness of planned invasion of the United Kingdom and, given its similarity to the Polish book, chillingly suggests what might have happened had the Battle of Britain been lost in 1940. Of the thousands of copies of the 'Nazi Black Book' reported to have been printed, this is one of only two known to have survived. It was given to the Library in late 1945 by the Ministry of Information, which had been accommodated in Senate House throughout World War II.

58.1 p. 32, with entries for Neville Chamberlain and Winston Churchill

58.1

22.6.36.

59.1

59.2

59 Senate House and the Tower under construction
1936–37

Photographic prints 229 × 287 mm,
mounted to 261 × 378 mm; UoL/CT/3/4/2

Fortnightly photographs recorded the construction of Senate House from 29 December 1932 to 11 October 1937. On 27 October 1936 the tower began to rise above Senate House (see fig. 59.2).

The tower was a key element in the programme for the building as devised by the University under the leadership of Sir William Beveridge. Vice-Chancellor from 1926, Beveridge had been the campaigning force behind the provision of a new headquarters for the University, with clear ideas about the new building. Whereas he characterised the Universities of Oxford and Cambridge as 'the type of the ancient English Universities, collegiate, residential, dropped as it were from heaven on two monkish mediaeval towns', London's new university building, by contrast, 'should be something that could not have been built in any earlier generation than this, and can only be at home in London'. Beveridge sought a building that would 'give London at its heart [...] a great architectural feature'. In particular, he hoped that the architect would think 'of at least one tower, with a great bell, a muezzin, calling the children of the University in all lands'.

The tower became a key test in the selection of the architect, Charles Holden. Holden saw Senate House as the culmination of his career, his masterpiece. But for many contemporaries it was an ambiguous masterpiece. London's first 'sky-scraper' was too modern and too vast for some; for others, not modernist enough. The photograph illustrates some of this ambiguity, showing at the top of the tower part of the steel frame which provides structure for the University Library's bookstacks: an innovative element but one concealed within traditional masonry. The photograph also shows one of the most sophisticated, and subtle, of Holden's modernist ideas. The windows on the third floor of Senate House follow a different rhythm from the windows on the floors below: a difference Holden, using jazz terminology, identified as syncopation, and one of the most unexpected modernist art forms to influence a university headquarters.

The University Archive shows how Holden developed his design in dialogue with the University, discussing the details which are an outstanding part of the building today, and debating the painting and sculpture that might or, in the case of Jacob Epstein, might not be included. Capturing the construction in photograph and film was part of the project to record all the formal and some of the informal acts of the University in preparing for its new Bloomsbury building.

59.1 construction of Senate House, 21 June 1936

59.2 construction of Senate House, 27 October 1936

59.3 construction of Senate House, 16 August 1937

59.3

| Eliot, Thomas Stearns | 28 | M.A. Harvard University. | 1. Tendencies of Contemporary French Thought (up to 1914 and after) 2. Contemporary French Poets and Novelists. 3. The Revolution and the Empire: a study of French Literature in Wartime. 4. Six Nineteenth Century Thinkers (Chateaubriand, Michelet, Ste-Beuve, Comte, Taine, Renan). 5. History of the Novel in France. 6. Literary Criticism in France. 7. Webster and other Followers of Shakespeare. 8. Contemporary Movements in English Literature. 10. Present Philosophical Tendencies. 11. Sociology of Primitive Peoples. 12. Social Psychology. | In Section B. of Oxford U.E. List. Tutor of Univ. Tutorial Class at Southall. | Postponed till Jan. 1915. Jan. 31, 1917. |
| 18 Crawford Mansions, Crawford St, W. | | | | | |

| Joad, Cyril Edwin Mitchinson | 27 | Balliol Coll Oxford John Locke Schol. in Mental & Moral Philosophy, 1914. First Class in Greats (Literas Humaniores) 1914. | See Yellow pamphlet for 1920 & 1921. | Short notes. | Lectured at working men's Coll, & for W.E.A. on Literature & Philosophy. Lectured for Fabian Society & Theosophical Society. | Political Philosophy of Robert Owen ("Robert Owen — Idealist": Fabian Tract). "Essays in Common Sense Philosophy" (Headley) Contributed an essay to "The Idea of Public Right" (Allen & Unwin). | Added to Panel, 1 October, 1919. Added to list of T.C. Tutors, 3 March, 1921. |

237   238

Name	Academic Qualifications	Courses offered	Read, or from Notes	Lecturing Experience	References	
DENHAM, Reginald (37) 21A Well Walk, Hampstead, N.W.3	[Producer of Plays in Lond. & New York.]	A short course of 4 lects. on Stage Production.	Short notes.	A series of lectures at Bristol University.	A. Compton-Rickett. Sir L. Ronald. Sir F. Benson. etc., etc.	Not added 12.1.32
GREAVES, Harold Richard Goring (23) 15 Edith Road, Kensington, W.14	B.Sc. (Econ.) (Lond.), 1929. 1st cl. hons. in Polit. Sci.	British Constitution. Internat. Government. Political Theory. League of Nations. French Political Thought since 1848.	Very short notes.	As Assist. Lect. at L.S. of E. since 1930.	H.J. Laski. H. Finer. Graham Wallas.	Postponed 12.1.32
GREENWOOD, Thomas (30) 7, Handel Mansions, W.C. 1	M.A. (Lond.), 1922, in Philosophy. L.-ès-L., (Paris) 1920.	Introd. to Scientific Philosophy. Changing Conceptions of the Universe.	Short notes.	As Lect. in Logic, Birkbeck Coll., since 1930. Lectures in various places e.g. Paris, Rome.	Dr G. Senter. C.E.M. Joad. Miss H. Oakeley	Not added 12.1.32
HART, Herbert Lionel Adolphus (24) 11, Primrose Hill Road, Chalk Farm, N.W.3	B.A. (Oxon.), 1929. 1st cl. Lit. Hum.	Roman provincial government in the Republic and Empire. Constitutional Ideas of Greeks and Romans. The Athenian Δεȣος of the Fifth Century.	Short notes.	None.	C.W.M. Cox. A.H. Smith. H.S. Jenkins. H.A.L. Fisher.	Not added 12.1.32
JEVONS, Herbert Stanley (56) Flat 11, 122, Southampton Row, W.C. 1	M.A. (Cantab.), B.Sc. (Lond.).	The Gold Standard and Foreign Exchange. India - its Polit. and Econ. Problems.	Short notes.	As Prof. of Econ. and Polit. Sci. in Univ. Coll., Cardiff, 1905-11. As Prof. of Econ. in Univ. of Allahabad, 1914-23. As Prof. of Econ. in Univ. of Rangoon, 1923-30. Frequent Ext. Courses in England and India.	_____	Added to Panel 12.1.32
LOESCH, Ronald Allison Ogden (24) 21 Walpole Street, S.W. 3	B.A. (Cantab.), 1929. 2nd and 3rd cl. hons. in the Econ. Tripos.	Capitalism v. Socialism. Causes of an Econ. Depression. A Mod. Philosophy of Religion. Social Forces in Mod. Lit.	Short notes.	Nil.	A. Compton-Rickett. K.W.M. Pickthorne. K. Fisher.	Not added 12.1.32
NICHOLS, Philip Peter Ross (29) 85, St. George's Square, S.W.1	M.A. (Cantab.), 1928. Hist. Trip. Pts I and II, 1st Div. 2nd cl.	Life, Art and Thought in the Ital. Renaissance. Mediaeval History. Form in Engl. Literature. The Art of Writing.	Usually from notes.	Lects. at City and Holl. Evg. Insts., 1931-32. School-teaching.	G.G. Coulton. Miss F. Beales. A.I. Ellis.	Not added 12.1.32

60 Notes by Barbara Wootton on prospective tutors
1938–44
UoL/EM/6/14
177 × 107 mm

The University of London played a pioneering role in opening up higher education to men and women of all social statuses and backgrounds. Its charter of 1858 paved the way by removing the link between registering for a degree and studying at a particular institution, thereby introducing the concept of distance learning. For the first time people could access a university education while remaining in their home and continuing to earn a living. The services offered by the Extra-Mural Department to British prisoners of war during World War II exemplified the flexibility afforded by this approach. Nobody was to be excluded from the pursuit of learning, however difficult their circumstances.

As befits such enlightened aims, the extra-mural programme was able to attract an extraordinary roster of tutors and lecturers. Quite how extraordinary is revealed by Barbara Wootton's notebook, containing comments on prospective tutors for the period 1938–44. Wootton herself, Director of Studies from 1927 to 1944, was a remarkable character. One of the first women to sit in the House of Lords, she was central to a number of the significant social and public policy reforms of the twentieth century. She was far from the only political figure to feature, and the Labour Party was particularly well represented at the University, from a future prime minister, Harold Wilson, to leader of the opposition Hugh Gaitskell. Away from politics, writers, composers and intellectuals were also prominent over the years, among them T. S. Eliot, Ralph Vaughan Williams, Millicent Fawcett and Sir Israel Gollancz, the founder of the British Academy.

The small blue notebook is evidence of the close interest that Wootton took in the vetting and hiring of tutors. She had a clear idea of what constituted 'the right type' and could be very dismissive of those who fell short of her standards: 'Hopeless', 'not our type', 'Rather dim. Unsuitable', 'Vague, but prob. adequate'. She responded well to the 'serious and thorough', 'very bright' and even the 'charming', but awarded most would-be tutors only cautious approval. Of Harold Wilson she wrote in April 1940: 'Pleasant, unassuming, a little academic. Has done no regular WEA [Workers' Educational Association] work […] Thinks of WEA as poss. career. Suitable: with experience'.

The indomitable Barbara Wootton's fascinating notebook reveals the records of the University of London's Extra-Mural Department as a rich source of information for historians not only of education but also of the cultural, political and social history of twentieth-century Britain.

60.4

60.1 UoL/EM/1/14, volume entitled 'Applications for lectureships', 1917: details of pp. 101–02, with note on extra-mural lecturer T. S. Eliot

60.2 UoL/EM/1/14, volume entitled 'Applications for lectureships', 1920: details of pp. 127–28, with note on extra-mural lecturer C. E. M. Joad

60.3 UoL/EM/1/14, volume entitled 'Applications for lectureships', 1932, pp. 237–38, with note on extra-mural lecturer H. S. Jevons

60.4 Barbara Wootton's notebook, showing entry for Harold Wilson

Further Reading

Bibliographical References

Adams = Adams, H. M., *Catalogue of Books Printed on the Continent of Europe, 1501–1600, in Cambridge Libraries*, 2 vols (London: Cambridge University Press, 1967)

Dartons = Darton, Lawrence, *The Dartons: An Annotated Check-List of Children's Books Issued by Two Publishing Houses, 1787–1876* (London: British Library, 2004)

GW = *Gesamtkatalog der Wiegendrucke* (Leipzig: Hiersemann, 1925–). Available at: http://www.gesamtkatalogderwiegendrucke.de/

ISTC = British Library, *Incunabula Short Title Catalogue*. Available at: http://istc.bl.uk/

Palau y Dulcet = Palau y Dulcet, Antonio, *Manual del Librero Hispano-Americano: Bibliografia General Espanola e Hispano-Americana desde la Invencion de la Imprenta Hasta Nuestros Tiempos, con el Valor Comercial de los Impresos Descritos*, 2nd edn, 28 vols (Barcelona: Palau, 1948–90)

STC = Pollard, A.W. and G. R. Redgrave, *A Short-Title Catalogue of Books Printed in England, Scotland, & Ireland and of English books Printed Abroad, 1475–1640*, 2nd edn, begun by W. A. Jackson and F. S. Ferguson, completed by K. F. Pantzer, 3 vols (London: Bibliographical Society, 1976–91)

Wing = Wing, Donald, *Short-Title Catalogue of Books Printed in England, Scotland, Ireland, Wales, and British America, and of English books Printed in Other Countries, 1641–1700*, 3 vols, 2nd edn (New York: Index Committee of the Modern Language Association of America, 1972–1988)

Further Reading (Collections)

Attar, K. E., 'Sir Edwin Durning-Lawrence: A Baconian and His Books', *The Library*, 7th ser., 5 (2004), pp. 294–315

—, 'Incunabula at Senate House Library: Growth of a Collection', *Library & Information History*, 25 (2009), pp. 97–116

—, 'The M.S. Anderson Collection of Writings on Russia Printed Between 1525 and 1917: An Introduction', *Solanus*, 22 (2011), pp. 63–78

'The Eliot-Phelips Collection: A Symposium to Celebrate the Cataloguing of a Unique Collection of Early Spanish Books, University of London Library and Institute of Romance Studies, 1998', *Journal of the Institute of Romance Studies*, 7 (1999), pp. 11–59

Pafford, J. H. P., 'Historical Introduction', in Margaret Canney and David Knott, *Catalogue of the Goldsmiths' Library of Economic Literature*, vol. 1, *Printed Books to 1800* (London: Athlone, 1981), pp. ix–xviii

'Private Libraries, XV: Sir Louis Sterling', *Times Literary Supplement* (4 Feb. 1939), p. 80

Walworth, Julia, 'Sir Louis Sterling and His Library', *Jewish Historical Studies*, 40 (2005), pp. 159–75

Further Reading (Treasures)

Attar, K. E., 'The Cowell Manuscript, or, The First Baconian: MS294 at the University of London', *Shakespeare Survey*, 65 (2012), 323–36 (no. 28)

Byron, George Gordon, *Lord Byron: 'Don Juan' Cantos X, XI, XII and XVII Manuscript: A Facsimile of the Original Draft Manuscripts in the University of London Library*, ed. Andrew Nicholson (New York and London: Garland, 1993) (no. 32)

Carlyle, Thomas, and Jane Welsh Carlyle, *The Collected Letters of Thomas and Jane Welsh Carlyle*, vol. 32: *October 1856–July 1857*, ed. Ian Campbell et al. (Durham, NC, and London: Duke University Press, 2004) (no. 43)

Duff, E. Gordon, *Printing in England in the Fifteenth Century: E. Gordon Duff's Bibliography with Supplementary Matter by Lotte Hellinga* (London: Bibliographical Society, 2009) (no. 7)

Grote, Harriet, *The Personal Life of George Grote*, 2nd edn (London: J. Murray, 1873) (no. 31)

Hellinga, Lotte, *Catalogue of Books Printed in the XVth Century Now in the British Library. Part XI: England* ('t Goy-Houten: HES & De Graaf, 2007) (no. 7)

Mosser, D. W., 'The Manuscript Glosses of the *Canterbury Tales* and the University of London's Copy of Pynson's [1492] Edition', *Chaucer Review*, 41 (2007), pp. 360–92 (no. 7)

Rye, Reginald Arthur, *Catalogue of the Manuscripts and Autograph Letters in the University Library at the Central Building of the University of London, South Kensington, S.W.3, with a Description of the Manuscript Life of Edward, Prince of Wales, the Black Prince by Chandos the Herald* (London: University of London Press, 1921) (no. 1)

Simpson, Richard, *The University of London's Senate House: Charles Holden, Classicism & Modernity* (London: University of London, 2005) (no. 59)

Turville-Petre, Thorlac, 'The Relationship of the Vernon and Clopton Manuscripts', in *Studies in the Vernon Manuscript*, ed. Derek Pearsall (Cambridge: D. S. Brewer, 1990), pp. 29–44 (no. 2)

Index

Until 2004, the central library of the
University of London was known as the
University of London Library. In 2004
it was renamed Senate House Library,
University of London.

Reference numbers are supplied for all
manuscripts and archival items featured.
The classmarks of printed books can be
found by consulting the Library's online
catalogue:
http://catalogue.ulrls.lon.ac.uk/search~S1

This edition © 2012 Scala Publishers Ltd
Text © 2012 Senate House Library,
except for entries 1–60 © 2012 the authors
Photography © 2012 Senate House Library

First published in 2012 by
Scala Publishers Ltd
Northburgh House
10 Northburgh St
London EC1V 0AT
Telephone: +44 (0) 20 7490 9900
www.scalapublishers.com

in association with Senate House Library

Hardback ISBN: 978-1-85759-790-5
Paperback ISBN: 978-1-85759-812-4

Editors: Christopher Pressler and Karen Attar
Project editor: Esme West
Copy editor: Matthew Taylor
Proof reader: Julie Pickard
Designer: Yvonne Dedman
Photographer: David Cooper
Printed and bound in Singapore

10 9 8 7 6 5 4 3 2 1

British Library Cataloguing in Publication Data

A catalogue record for this book is available
from the British Library.

Front cover: details of (clockwise from top left)
nos. 1, 3, 3, 15, 13, 10, 19, 40, 36, 50, 18 and 11

Back cover: UoL/SV/V/36, Senate House and Library
from the south-west by night, *c.* 1938

Endpapers: detail from UoL/ST/1/1/4, University of
London Third Charter, 1858, which enabled students
throughout the British Empire, whether or not they
were at an affiliated institution, to gain a University
of London degree

Half-title: detail of *The Fables of Esope* (Newton:
Greynog Press), p. 4, 'The dog and the sheep'

Frontispiece: The Works of Geoffrey Chaucer
(Hammersmith: Kelmscott Press, 1896), p. 1

Arts of the Degrees hereby authorized to be conferred by the said University of London...

regulations in that behalf shall from time to time determine such regulations being subject to the pre...

37 **And** for the purpose of granting the Degrees of Bachelor of Medicine and Doctor of Medicine and for...

...ctments **We do further hereby Will and Ordain** that the said Chancellor Vice...

appear to them to be the Medical Institutions and Schools from which either singly or jointly to...

the judgment of the said Chancellor Vice Chancellor and Fellows to admit Candidates for Medical De...

for the respective Degrees of Bachelor of Medicine or Doctor of Medicine to be conferred by the sa...

have in any one or more of such Institutions or Schools completed the course of instruction which...

shall be lawful for the said Chancellor Vice Chancellor and Fellows from time to time with the appro...

any of the said Institutions or Schools included therein or by adding others thereunto

38 **And We further Will and ordain** that the said Chancellor Vice Chancellor and Fellows...

Medicine Music and also in such other departments of knowledge except Theology as the said Chan...

that such reasonable fees shall be charged for the Degrees so conferred as the said Chancellor Vice Cha...

39 **And We further Will and ordain** that at the conclusion of every examination of the Candi...

the said Degrees together with such particulars as the said Chancellor Vice Chancellor and Fellows shall...

University of London and signed by the said Chancellor or in his absence or incapacity by the Vice Chancellor...

Vice Chancellor and Fellows shall seem fitting to be stated therein —

40 **And We further Will and ordain** that the said Chancellor Vice Chancellor and Fe...

shall not without the consent of Convocation in each case entitle the holder thereof to be or become a Me...

41 **And We further Will and ordain** that the said Chancellor Vice Chancellor and Fellows...

Chancellor Vice Chancellor and Fellows shall from time to time by regulations made in that behalf determine...

said Chancellor Vice Chancellor and Fellows may cause to be held from time to time examinations of persons...

of proficiency as aforesaid subject to such regulations as by the said Chancellor Vice Chancellor and Fe...

examined by Examiners appointed by the said Chancellor Vice Chancellor and Fellows and at the...

whom they shall have seemed to be entitled to any such Certificate together with such particulars as...

the said Chancellor a Certificate under the seal of the said University of London and signed by the said Chan...

in respect of which he has obtained the Certificate shall be stated together with such other particulars...

fees shall be charged for such Certificates of proficiency as the said Chancellor Vice Chancellor and Fellows...

42 **And We further Will and ordain** that all fees shall be carried to one general fee fund...

Treasury to follow the Accounts of income and expenditure of the University shall once in every year be submitted...

43 **Provided always** that all regulations made from time to time in relation to any of the matt...

and countersigned by them as by Our said Charter provided.

44 **And lastly We do** hereby for Us our heirs and successors **grant and declare**...

and effectual in the law according to the true intent and meaning of the same And shall be const...

elsewhere notwithstanding any nonrecital misrecital uncertainty or imperfection in these Our Let...

Witness Ourself at Our Palace at Westminster this ninth day of April in...

By Her Majesty